WILLIAM BLAKE

THE GATES
OF PARADISE

WILLIAM BLAKE

—

THE GATES
OF PARADISE

MICHAEL BEDARD

Tundra Books

Copyright © 2006 by Michael Bedard

Published in Canada by Tundra Books,
75 Sherbourne Street, Toronto, Ontario M5A 2P9

Published in the United States by Tundra Books of Northern New York,
P.O. Box 1030, Plattsburgh, New York 12901

Library of Congress Control Number: 2006902490

Library and Archives Canada Cataloguing in Publication

Bedard, Michael, 1949-
   William Blake : the gates of paradise / Michael Bedard.

Includes bibliographical references and index.
ISBN 13: 978-0-88776-763-0
ISBN 10: 0-88776-763-X

   1. Blake, William, 1757-1827 – Juvenile literature.   2. Poets, English – 18th century –
Biography – Juvenile literature.   3. Poets, English – 19th century – Biography – Juvenile
literature.   4. Artists – Great Britain – Biography – Juvenile literature.   I. Title.
II. Title: Gates of paradise.

PR4146.B34 2006   j821'.7   C2006-901706-9

We acknowledge the financial support of the Government of Canada through the Book
Publishing Industry Development Program (BPIDP) and that of the Government of Ontario
through the Ontario Media Development Corporation's Ontario Book Initiative. We further
acknowledge the support of the Canada Council for the Arts and the Ontario Arts Council
for our publishing program.

ONTARIO ARTS COUNCIL
CONSEIL DES ARTS DE L'ONTARIO

Design: Sean Tai
Typeset in Minion

Printed and bound in Canada

1 2 3 4 5 6   11 10 09 08 07 06

Mostly Martha

"Labour well the Minute Particulars, attend to the Little-ones,
And those who are in misery cannot remain so long
If we but do our duty: labour well the teeming earth."

From *Jerusalem*

ACKNOWLEDGMENTS

The roots of this book reach back forty years, when a kind teacher took a young poet under her wing and, along with encouraging him in the craft, introduced him to the work of William Blake. To that teacher, Marilyn Joiner, I am eternally grateful.

I am grateful, too, to the many scholars whose work has helped illumine the life and work of Blake for me, and whose influence is to be felt in every line of this book. Among these, I am indebted in a special way to G.E. Bentley, Jr., a formidable scholar and a tireless champion of Blake who, with kindness and generosity, has supported and encouraged this project through its long gestation. I am thankful for the hospitality that he and his wife, Elizabeth Budd Bentley, have shown me.

I am grateful to the Victoria University Library and, in particular, Robert Brandeis for making items from the G.E. Bentley, Jr. Blake Collection available to me in a time of transition; to Robert Essick, Joseph Viscomi, and the Blake Archive for their help in providing images from their collection; and to the Rare Book and Special Collections Division of the Library of Congress for their profound generosity in making available images from the Rosenwald Collection for this project.

As an unrepentant Luddite, I am thankful for the assistance of Bambi Rutledge and Mary-Anne Bedard in dealing with the world onscreen in the matter of acquiring images. I am grateful to my agent, Linda McKnight, for her guidance.

My thanks, as always, to the staff at Tundra Books: to Kathy Lowinger for her ongoing support, to Lauren Bailey for her invaluable assistance in bringing together the images for this book, and to Sue Tate for her fine editing skills.

But my thanks go mostly to my dear wife, Martha. Without her love and support, none of this would be.

CONTENTS

THE COCOONED CHILD

WHAT IS MAN?

A cocoon on an oak leaf, though certainly no ordinary cocoon. Rather a vision of a cocoon as a child in swaddling clothes, asleep. And below it a question, "What is Man?"

This mysterious picture is the frontispiece to a little book called *The Gates of Paradise*, engraved and printed by William Blake in 1793. It is what is known as an emblem book, composed of symbolic pictures meant to rouse the reader's imagination to unfold their meaning.

The Gates of Paradise contains seventeen such pictures, with brief mottoes beneath. They chart the inner journey of a life from birth through death. You will find one of these little pictures at the head of each chapter here.

According to its title page, *The Gates of Paradise* was a book "For Children," and it is perhaps children, or those who still see with the eyes of a child, who can best unfold the mystery of its images.

William Blake was born into an age in tumult, an age that saw the birth of the industrial revolution. He was an engraver by trade, a craftsman in an age that no longer valued craft. He was a visionary in an age that had no time for visions. This was the age of the machine, the rise of industry, and the spread of factories. The winners were few and the losers many.

Blake witnessed the dark side of the industrial revolution. He saw what the introduction of steam-powered machinery and the rise of the factory system had done to the lives of ordinary men, women, and children. He saw the sufferings of the poor and the oppressed. He saw that a devotion to materialist beliefs withered the human spirit and left people feeling impotent and alone, adrift in a mechanical universe.

Blake was not simply an engraver; he was a poet and a painter. He dreamt of uniting the arts of writing and painting, as the artists of the Middle Ages had in their illuminated manuscripts. He discovered a way to write and draw on the copper plates he used for engraving, and create a raised image he could print from on his wooden press and then color by hand.

He called his discovery Illuminated Printing, and in the books he created with it, he confronted all systems of power that confined the human spirit. He announced a gospel of freedom and fellowship founded on the exercise of the creative imagination. In a world impressed with the great and powerful, he celebrated the small. He delighted in the innocence of the child. He showed us "a world in a grain of sand, and a heaven in a wild flower."

There is that in us that craves to open and bloom and bear fruit. We are at our best when we are bringing out that small thing within us, when we are exercising our imagination – when we are creating. Perhaps this is the meaning of the cocooned child asleep on the oak leaf. We are much more than "worms of sixty winters." We are creatures that can grow and transform and break free of the things that bind us. "In every bosom a universe expands as wings," wrote Blake. This is the story of the universe that opened in him and struggled to be free.

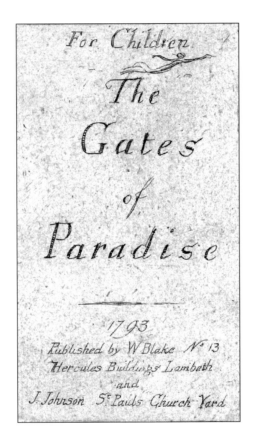

GOLDEN SQUARE

By 1800 the population of London approached one million, making it the largest city in the Western world. The sheer size was overwhelming. It was a vast forest of brick, a bewildering labyrinth of streets and lanes, of narrow alleys and dim courts.

It was a city of incredible contrasts. In the shadows of the luxurious neighborhoods where the wealthy lived stood the wretched hovels where the poor eked out a precarious existence. The population of London had soared through the eighteenth century as legions of dispossessed farmers and rural craftsmen flocked to the city. Buildings were thrown up haphazardly to accommodate the influx. Large families were crammed into ramshackle rooms. The poorest lived in garrets and cellars, the openings of which were set into the street. At night the cellar-dwellers would leave their doors open to let in the air, and those walking the streets in the dark had to be wary of falling down the holes.

Refuse and sewage ran along gutters in the street, and the foul odor mingled with the stench of sweat as people thronged the narrow passages. The smoke of coal fires plumed from a sea of chimneys and hung like a pall over the teeming city, blackening the buildings with soot.

The din of the city could be heard from a great distance off – a noise not of machines, but of clamoring voices vying with one another: street vendors at their tumbledown stalls, crying their wares; hawkers and peddlers selling bread and meat, fruit and fish, each with his or her own distinctive cry.

Life for most Londoners was desperately uncertain. Even the shopkeepers' trade was insecure. Work was often seasonal, and in the off-season many families fell into debt and were thrown upon the mercy of the parish. Beggars and abandoned children wandered the streets day and night, lurking in the shadows of doorways, living however they could.

London at Night, *1760. A link-boy with a torch guides a gentleman through the darkened streets.*

Bloomsbury Square, 1787. The wealthy promenade around their spacious squares.

In the midst of this sea of disorder stood islands of affluence, which took the form of squares – rows of houses built around an open green space. Here the wealthy led their ordered lives. The first square built in London was Covent Garden in 1631, and by Blake's day, there were numerous squares scattered through the West End of the city, home to the aristocracy and the gentry. These were their "town houses." Most had country estates, where they spent much of their time.

It was the Age of Reason, and order reigned supreme through all facets of polite society. Manners were formal and precise. In the arts, painting proceeded according to rational principles; poetry aimed at the ideals of regularity and rhyme. The universe itself was thought of as a vast, well-oiled machine.

The houses of the rich were spacious and uniform, built around large, fenced-in plots of grass where gravel paths wound. Here ladies of fashion and their gentlemen

6

Golden Square, 1754. A statue of King James stands in the center of the square, surrounded by a grass plot, a gravel walk, and a wooden fence.

enjoyed promenading in their finery, seeing and being seen. They posted servants at the entrances to ensure that none of the "inferior sort" were allowed in.

In the parish of St. James stood one such square. It was called Golden Square, built in the 1680s by the famous architect Christopher Wren, on land just south of an area known as Pesthouse Close. During the plague years, this had been the site of a hospital for the infected and a vast plague pit for the victims. It was an unsavory site on which to build, but land was at a premium, and the press of polite society to the fashionable West End was unstoppable.

Over time, a grid of straight, wide streets grew around the square. Here small businesses set up shop, catering to the tastes of their wealthy neighbors. One of these streets, named Broad Street because of its width, pushed out into Pesthouse Close. It is here our story begins.

7

CHAPTER ONE

A VISIONARY BOY

I FOUND HIM BENEATH A TREE

N THE EVENING OF NOVEMBER 28, 1757, JAMES BLAKE EMERGED from his hosiery and haberdashery shop at 28 Broad Street and lit the parish lamp that hung in front of it. The lamp was a simple affair – a tin vessel filled with fish oil, a cotton twist for a wick, enclosed in a semiopaque glass case. It was the law that, on moonless nights, shopkeepers must light their lamps at dusk for the safety of passersby.

The windows of the shop were lit as well. Samples of his wares were on display – gloves and stockings, hats and caps, assorted frills and notions. Normally the shop was open late, but on this night James Blake decided to close early. Today was a special day, for in the rooms above the shop, where he and his family lived, his wife, Catherine, had just given birth to their third child, a baby boy.

28 Broad Street, the Blake family home (now known as Broadwick St.). The building was torn down in 1959.

Two weeks later, they took the infant to the local parish church – St. James, Picadilly – and christened him William. Apart from christening their children there, the Blakes likely had little to do with such grand churches, for they, along with many London shopkeepers and craftsmen, were what was known as Dissenters.

The state religion was the Church of England, and the monarch was its head. It had its churches, such as St. James, its liturgy, its traditions. It cast its nets wide, but it did not gather all. Those who chose to worship in other ways were known as Nonconformists or Dissenters and were generally viewed by the ruling class with some suspicion. For radical political views often went hand in hand with religious dissent.

There were a host of Dissenting sects in the London of that time. While it is impossible to say to which of them the Blakes belonged, it is possible that they "attended the Moravian Chapel in Fetter Lane." Catherine Blake had been a member of the Moravian congregation in a previous marriage, and she and her new family may have continued to worship with them.

The Moravians were a joyful and fearless people. Their roots were in Europe, where they had experienced fierce persecution. The initial members were mostly peasants and craftsmen, who practised a simple faith based on right conduct and the common good. They followed the spirit's lead in all things, and considered all people equal before God. They wrote many hymns, for much of their worship consisted of song, which brought their beliefs within reach of simple people. Though small in number, they stood in the forefront of the modern Protestant missionary movement. They felt themselves called to minister to those overlooked or neglected by others. In 1735 they came to England, and established the church at Fetter Lane three years later.

Family worship was important to the Dissenters, and William was raised in an atmosphere of religious enthusiasm and love of the Bible. His mother likely sang to him the simple hymns she knew so well. These things stayed with him. All his life long he had an abiding concern for the lowly of the earth, a love of song, and a deep attachment to the Bible.

※

William's parents saw that this child was different from an early age. He was a dreamer, and he possessed a powerful imagination.

One day, a customer in the shop was talking about a beautiful city he had seen on a recent journey. "Do you call that splendid?" piped up William, who had been listening intently. "I should call a city splendid in which the houses were of gold, the pavement of silver, and the gates ornamented with precious stones."

He may have read of such a wondrous city in the descriptions of the New Jerusalem in his Bible, but he clearly saw it in his imagination. So vividly did he see such things that there were times when the boundaries between that inner world and the everyday world became blurred. Once, when he was just four, he set the whole house in a flurry by screaming out that he had seen God put his face to the window.

Not only was their strange son highly imaginative, but he also loved to draw. It was probably his mother who first put paper and pencil in his hands, for from the time he was three, he was always drawing. Soon the walls of her room were filled with the pictures he had drawn for her, many of them accompanied by poems he had written.

Neither William nor the rest of the Blake children were sent to school. Like many Dissenters, the Blakes were suspicious of education outside their sect. William was taught the basics of reading and writing at his mother's knee. She saw to it that there were books at hand for him to read, and beyond that left him to follow his own course. It was the greatest gift she could have given him. His spelling and punctuation suffered because of it, but his talents flourished. Years later, he wrote

Thank God I never was sent to school
To be Flogd into following the Style of a Fool.

The Blake family continued to grow. By the time William was six, he had three brothers and a baby sister. The children's bedrooms were likely on the top floor of the house, and from an early age the children were set to work doing small jobs around the shop. William was soon busy sweeping up, wrapping parcels, helping customers with their purchases, and fetching and delivering for his father.

As he began to explore the neighborhood, he discovered a city quite unlike the city of gold he saw in his imagination. The streets here were paved not with silver but with cobblestone, and not everyone wore such fine clothes or lived in such fine houses as the ladies from Golden Square who came to his father's shop.

On the far side of the same block where his family lived stood the St. James parish workhouse, home to over three hundred poor souls, many of them children no older than William. It was a bleak place, set on the grounds of an old cemetery that ran almost directly behind the Blakes' shop. Though the cemetery was full, poor-holes were still being dug there. It was a short trip from the workhouse to the graveyard for those who failed to survive the rigors of workhouse life. The poor-holes were left partially uncovered, and the stench that arose in sultry weather was a source of constant complaint in the neighborhood.

Then, too, just around the corner and up the street from the shop stood the Carnaby Market slaughterhouse, a foul shambles famous for its female butchers. Rich and poor, high and low, rubbed shoulders in the streets the young boy came to know. But where was the city of gold that he had imagined?

William drew everything, everywhere, sketching the likenesses of what he saw, making copies of the prints that hung on the walls of the shop. Drawing and imagining went hand in hand with him.

His father would set him at the counter of the shop to tally up a bill. But William had no head for figures; he would end up drawing on the back of the bill and doodling on the counter. Finally, despairing that the boy would ever follow in his footsteps, his father let him find his own way.

Often then, young William, freed from his shop duties, went off on his own, his pockets crammed with paper and pencils, a book tucked under his arm. He loved to wander. As he grew older, he was allowed to range freely. By the time he was eight or nine, he was making his way from the busy city streets to the Surrey countryside, south of the city across the river. He would simply walk on and on, until London lay far behind and he was alone on the winding lanes in the midst of rolling fields. He loved this solitary walking more than anything in the world. Away from the noise of the city and the shop, and sums that never worked out, he was free – to dream, to imagine to his heart's content. Here, in the midst of these green fields, if he imagined hard enough, he could see that city of gold rising in splendor, the narrow lane becoming a street of silver, the gates of precious stones swinging open before him.

And so we can imagine this short, squarely built boy sauntering along in the summer heat, with his shock of reddish hair standing out from his head like forks of flame, and his large eyes looking intently at everything, sometimes almost seeming to look through things.

And then one day, as he walked along absorbed in his thoughts, he glanced up and saw a tree – a tree full of angels. They were sitting on the boughs, their bright wings flashing in the sun. He ran home as fast as he could and told his parents.

His father was not amused. He was a kind and gentle man, but he had no patience with lying, and when the boy refused to back down, he threatened to beat him. Only his mother's intervention spared William the blows.

But the boy knew he had not lied, nor had he merely imagined. He had *seen*. It was among the first of what he came to call "my visions." There would be more, mostly in the countryside at first, when he was walking alone. Like the time he saw the angels moving among the haymakers, or the prophet Ezekiel standing under a tree.

In time he would come to speak of his visions in the matter-of-fact way that we speak of everyday things, but for now he felt it wiser to keep them to himself.

CHAPTER TWO

THE YOUNG APPRENTICE

WATER

 HEN HE WAS TEN YEARS OLD, WILLIAM'S PARENTS ENROLLED their gifted son in Pars Drawing School, a popular school for young artists situated in a house in the Strand, about a mile from the Blakes' home. The fees at the school were high, but the Blakes lived in a neighborhood of artists and they no doubt saw that a boy with such gifts, if properly trained, could both do the thing he loved and make a respectable living too.

It was a wise decision. William's natural gift was now given direction. At the school, young students learned the basics of drawing by copying prints of famous paintings and sketching plaster casts of Greek and Roman statues. His father bought him small models of these statues, which he could copy at home.

At this time in England, there were no public art galleries. Most original

works of art were owned by noblemen and rich gentlemen, a few of whom permitted select members of the public into their homes to view their private collections – for a fee. Schoolboys were not usually considered select members, but the Duke of Richmond opened his doors to the students of Pars school and allowed them to draw in his gallery. And so, at an early age, William saw how the wealthy lived.

As he well knew, not everyone lived so. The shocking difference between the lives of the rich and the poor was everywhere apparent. Sometimes desperation drove the poor to crime, and even petty theft was punishable by death. It was the rich who made the laws and they guarded their property fervently.

Popular unrest against an unjust system led increasingly to rioting. In these spontaneous uprisings, the individual was to some degree protected by the crowd. The most common reason for rioting was the price of bread.

The city poor were utterly dependent on the fair price of staples such as bread in order to survive. Any sudden sharp increase in price was enough to spark spontaneous rioting. In rallying the mob, one of the leaders would raise a loaf of bread, draped in black cloth and inscribed with a slogan such as "Famine decked in sackcloth," aloft on a pole before the crowd.

In the spring of 1768, a year after William had entered Pars Drawing School, one such riot took place. The following March, merchants who had opposed the rioters attempted to present a petition of support to the king. The mob attacked their coaches, pelting them with mud and stones and harassing them until many were forced to turn back. All the shops in the neighborhood, including the Blakes' haberdashery shop on Broad Street, were forced to close.

⚜

A small shopkeeper such as William's father was certainly better off than many, but life was still precarious, and maintaining a business and raising a family were not easy. Yet he continued to fund his artistic child's education and more.

At twelve, William was receiving enough spending money to buy prints of his own. He eagerly haunted print shops and auction houses. The small boy,

with his unruly hair, must have made a strange sight among the genteel print collectors.

The auctioneer Langford took a liking to the boy. He called him his "little connoisseur." Even at this early age, William's tastes were already decided. He favored the Renaissance masters, artists who had fallen out of fashion. So when he placed small bids on old prints by Raphael, Michelangelo, and Dürer, the kindly auctioneer would quickly close the bidding so that the items would go to the boy.

Back home, William would pore over his prints, copying and recopying his favorites. "To learn the Language of Art, 'Copy for Ever' is my Rule," he would later write. He hung the walls of his room with his work, and, in the evenings, he read the books he had selected from bookstalls and dealers' shops at bargain prices. He loved the poets – Shakespeare and Spenser, Milton and Donne. He read, made notes in the margins, and began to write poems of his own to imitate those he admired.

At fourteen, he finished his studies at the drawing school and was faced with the question of what to do next. He could be trained as a painter, but the fees for lessons from a reputable artist were high. It did not seem fair to burden his family with such an expense.

William suggested to his parents that he become an apprentice to an engraver instead. After all, the prints he had so passionately collected and copied were engravings. Why shouldn't he learn the art himself? He could both pursue his artistic studies and be taught a skilled trade.

It was a momentous decision, with enduring consequences.

❧

William and his father first visited the studio of engraver William Ryland. Ryland had studied in France and brought back to England the fashionable stipple style of engraving, a style that emphasized softness and tone rather than line. His work became immensely popular, and he was appointed Engraver to the King. Ryland was able to command a high fee for taking on a

new apprentice, but James Blake was willing to pay it to establish his son in such influential company.

But, secretly, all was not well with William Ryland. Some months before, his lucrative print-selling business had gone bankrupt, and he was in shocking financial trouble. Some inkling of this must have struck young William, for as they left the studio, he turned to his father and said, "I do not like that man's face. It looks as if he will live to be hanged."

Eleven years later, in August 1783, William Wynne Ryland suffered the dubious distinction of being the last man hanged on Tyburn Tree, convicted of forging checks on the East India Company for over seven thousand pounds.

William's strange forebodings were enough to persuade his father to look elsewhere. They called next at the studio of James Basire, a distinguished antiquarian engraver. His shop was just half a mile from the Blakes' own, at 31 Great Queen Street. Basire was the polar opposite of William Ryland. He was of the old school of engraving, a style grounded in drawing and dedicated to the "firm and determinate outline." This style had fallen out of fashion in favor of the smooth style of Ryland and his admirers. But William was drawn to the older, more formal style, for that was the style of Michelangelo and Dürer, the masters whose prints he had so eagerly collected and copied.

And so it was that on August 4, 1772, at fourteen, William Blake became apprenticed to James Basire, engraver to the Society of Antiquaries and the Royal Society. In a signed document, James Blake agreed to pay James Basire fifty-two pounds, while Basire promised to teach his new apprentice the "Art and Mystery" of his craft, and to feed, house, and clothe him for seven years.

If Basire abided by his promise, he was among the minority of masters at the time. The apprentice system, which dated back to ancient times, was clearly on the decline in eighteenth-century London. "Out-door apprentices" were increasingly common as masters ignored the residency requirement and simply locked their apprentices out of the shop when they closed for the day. With little or no money and no place to go, young apprentices fell into bad company, formed rowdy gangs, and roamed the streets by night.

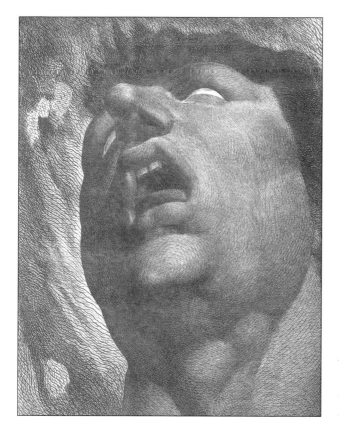

Head of a Damned Soul,
engraved by Blake from an
original work by Fuseli, 1787.
A stunning example of the
intricate network of lines the
engraver used to create shape
and tone.

Basire turned out to be kindly and doubtless took his young apprentice under his wing. Traditionally, an apprentice was expected to bed down in a corner of the shop, or under the shop counter. But the Basire family occupied a large house above their shop, and William may have been given a small room of his own, where he could hang his prints on the wall and keep his books on a shelf by his bed.

For the next seven years, he worked twelve hours a day, six days a week, returning home on Sundays to visit his family. He learned the exacting, arduous craft of the engraver thoroughly.

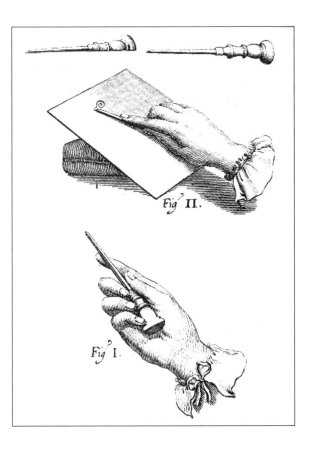

An illustration from an early engraving manual showing how to hold the graver.

In those days, engraving and etching were the only means of reproducing paintings and drawings as prints or book illustrations. The task of the engraver was to transfer the image to a copper plate by cutting a network of lines in the plate to represent the shapes and tones of the original. The tool used for this was the graver. Bending close to the metal plate, cutting line after line for hours on end was painstaking work, hatching and crosshatching until the image looked as if it were wound in an intricate web.

As a new apprentice, William would have first been taught more basic skills – how to hammer the plates smooth and carefully clean and polish them; to sharpen the gravers on a whetstone; to mix the oily black printer's ink and roll it smooth on a marble slab; to dampen and press the paper to be used in printing.

Only after he had thoroughly mastered these skills would he have been taught to use the graver. He would have been shown how to hold the knob in the palm of his hand while resting his forefinger along the top of the blade. The line was engraved by pressing the sharp, diamond-shaped point down into the copper and pushing it away from you. By changing the angle of the blade, you could make the cut broad or narrow. As the blade plowed through the copper, a thin curl of metal formed before it, which was carefully removed.

While working on the plate, you rested it on a leather pad full of sand. A curved line was created by slowly revolving the plate on the pad while keeping the graver rigid. It was slow, intense work, requiring not only a keen eye but considerable physical strength.

Once the engraving was complete, you thoroughly inked the plate, making sure that the ink was pressed into all the engraved lines. Then you wiped the surface of the plate clean with a rag, so that only the engraved lines held the ink.

A sheet of damp paper was then laid over it, and over that, a woolen cloth called a blanket. The whole was passed under pressure through the rollers of a hand press, forcing the paper deep into the inked lines and the ink into the paper. Finally, the completed print was hung to dry.

Slowly, over the course of his apprenticeship, William became skilled in each of these tasks. They were skills that would serve him well his whole life long. For it was as an engraver that he would earn his livelihood. In his lifetime he would make close to five hundred commercial engravings.

For a period of two years, things went along smoothly at the shop. And then Basire took on a new apprentice, one James Parker. Later he and William would become friends and business partners, but now the two quarreled constantly. To restore peace to the shop, Basire sent his talented young draftsman out each day to work on a job for him at Westminster Abbey. The Society of Antiquaries had commissioned Basire to make engravings of the many monuments of

The effigy of Henry III by Blake c. 1774, one of the portraits he made from the funeral monuments in Westminster Abbey.

kings and queens that were clustered in the Abbey. Basire so respected William's abilities that he entrusted him with the task of making the drawings from which the engravings would be copied.

For the next several years, William spent much of his time working alone in the vast old church, with its high vaulted ceilings, its narrow passageways, its chapels and cloisters and crypts. It was a world of stone, steeped in history. Rumors of that past clung here and there to the walls as patches of gilt and paint that had once adorned the whole. Here, "he found a treasure which he knew how to value."

William was to make sketches of the royal monuments crowded into the chapel of Edward the Confessor. Like figures asleep in the stone, life-sized effigies of the dead kings and queens lay atop the large marble tombs that held their bones. He sketched each one precisely, as if he were drawing a portrait. At times he stood astride the tombs or on scaffolding to view the figures from above.

Months stretched into years, as he breathed in the Gothic air of the old church. His imagination fed upon the place, shaping him forever. The curving lines, the elongated figures, the muted richness of color that he came to love in the art of the Abbey infused his later work.

One day, as William was perched on his scaffold lost in his drawing, he was interrupted by a group of boys from Westminster School, loitering about the Abbey between classes. They began to poke fun at the studious young artist bent over his work. When William ignored them, one of the boys scaled a pinnacle on a level with the scaffolding, the better to taunt him. Finally, William had enough. He sprang up and pushed the boy from his perch, sending him sprawling to the chapel floor. From then on, the boys were locked out of the Abbey except during services.

Often enough, William found himself as wholly alone in the vast old church as he had been on his long walks in the country. And, as the visions had come to him there, so did they here. One day, while he was busy drawing, he had a sudden vision of Christ and his apostles strolling among the tombs. And another time, as he worked in the stillness of the chapel, he heard chanting from the empty church, and when he went to investigate, saw a visionary procession of ancient monks, priests, and choristers passing solemnly along the shadowed aisles.

In the spring of 1774, William was present at a more mundane but equally remarkable event. Members of the society that had commissioned William's drawings obtained royal permission to open the tomb of King Edward I, and Basire entrusted his young apprentice to record what they found.

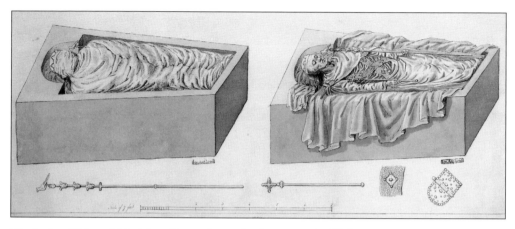

The body of Edward I in his coffin, as drawn by the apprentice Blake, 1774.

According to historical records, when the king died in 1307, he had been embalmed. The purpose of opening the tomb now was to inspect the condition of the body. When the heavy lid was raised and the wrappings removed, the body was discovered to be perfectly preserved, dressed in regal robes, a crown upon its head, the twin scepters still held in its hands. The skin had darkened to a deep brown, and though the features were somewhat shrunken, they had not decayed. Young William made two quick sketches of the body before it crumbled into dust and the tomb was resealed.

During the winter months, when it grew too cold to work in the Abbey, William returned to the studio to engrave the portraits he had sketched. In his spare time, he drew and engraved subjects of his own. His earliest original engraving dates from this period, entitled *Joseph of Arimathea Among the Rocks of Albion.*

The figure, he notes, is "from an old Italian Drawing," in fact, an engraving from a painting by Michelangelo. But William placed the figure into an English setting and transformed him into the legendary Joseph of Arimathea, who was believed to have carried the gospel message to England along with the Holy Grail, and to have founded the first English church at Glastonbury.

Joseph of Arimathea Among the Rocks of Albion,
first engraved by Blake at fifteen, revised as here c. 1810.

Years later, when he re-engraved the plate, William added the following explanatory note beneath the figure: "This is one of the Gothic artists who built the Cathedrals in what we call the Dark Ages, Wandering about in sheep skins and goat skins, of whom the world was not worthy . . ."

Perhaps young William Blake saw something of himself in this solitary figure standing at the edge of the sea, contemplating the high calling that lay before him.

CHAPTER THREE

STRUGGLING INTO BUSINESS

EARTH

IS APPRENTICESHIP COMPLETED, WILLIAM MOVED BACK IN with his family and set about earning his living as a journeyman engraver. It must have been a shock to trade the vast spaces of Westminster Abbey for the close confines of the family home, the quiet work of engraving monuments for the bustle of the publishing business, where a young engraver must find what work he could. It probably weighed heavily on him that trivial commissions for the magazine and book trade were likely now to be his lot.

And so, to further his artistic training, William applied to be a student at the Royal Academy. He submitted one of his drawings, and a letter of reference from an established artist, perhaps his former master, James Basire. Upon

Students drawing from life at the Royal Academy.

completing a large anatomical drawing, at least two feet high and fully labeled, he was accepted into the Academy in October 1779 to study as an engraver. He was issued an ivory ticket, which entitled him to attend classes and lectures for six years. Instruction was free, but students were expected to provide their own materials. Since classes were held in the late afternoon, William could still attempt to earn his living as an engraver during the day.

The Royal Academy had been formed a little over ten years before to promote a national art based on classical ideals. Students began by copying plaster casts of antique Greek sculptures, and proceeded to life studies. William was never a believer in drawing from life. "Natural objects always did weaken, deaden and obliterate Imagination in me," he would later write. His ideals in art had been shaped by the old prints he had pored over as a boy and by the figures he had spent so many years sketching at the Abbey. At twenty-one, his opinions were already formed, and once he had formed an opinion he was not easily moved from it.

Soon William collided with the establishment artists who ran the Academy. He clashed with George Moser, the Keeper, who was in charge of running the day-to-day operations. "I was once looking over prints from Raphael and Michelangelo in the Library of the Royal Academy," Blake later remembered. "Moser came to me and said: 'You should not study these old Hard, Stiff and Dry, Unfinished Works of Art – Stay a little and I will show you what you should study.'"

Moser fetched portfolios of engravings by the more modern artists Le Brun and Rubens.

William wanted none of it. Finally, he lashed out: "These things you call Finished are not even Begun. How can they then be Finished? The Man who does not know the Beginning never can know the End of Art."

We can imagine the seventy-four-year-old Moser's reaction to this upstart young engraver. Even though the Academy accepted engravers such as William as students, they always considered them inferiors, mere copiers rather than real artists.

Class divisions were rigid, and because he earned his living as a reproductive engraver, William fell into the class of skilled craftsmen. And so, from the very outset, his station in life was set.

One day he showed some of his work to Sir Joshua Reynolds, President of the Academy. Reynolds was an oil painter and a portraitist much sought after by the rich and famous. He looked at the young engraver's designs and told him he should work with less extravagance and more simplicity. In other words, he should strive to be more conventional. It must have been painfully clear to William that the treasures of imagination he had discovered in Westminster Abbey were considered mere extravagance in the halls of the Royal Academy.

Yet there was one teacher at the Academy with whom William did find himself in sympathy – the Irishman James Barry. Barry shared the young artist's passion for the Italian masters Michelangelo and Raphael. He had returned to England from a stay in Italy, fired with the idea of creating British paintings on the same scale as Michelangelo's massive designs for the ceiling of the Sistine Chapel.

From 1777 to 1783, Barry devoted all his energies to painting large murals of historical subjects on the walls of the Great Room at the Royal Society of Arts. During that time he received precious little encouragement from the Society for the Encouragement of Art. He was paid a pittance and later told Blake that he had been forced to live on bread and apples while he completed the commission.

Barry was appointed Professor of Painting while William was a student at the Royal Academy. The young artist attended his lectures and was inspired by Barry's vision of a golden age of art, which he believed had flourished in ancient times. Here, clearly, was someone who honored the past with the same passion as William himself.

Barry was always something of an outsider. Eventually he ran afoul of the Academy and the politics that governed it, and was dismissed in 1799. His final years were spent living a near-reclusive existence in a ruined house near Cavendish Square, the target of abuse by the neighborhood children who threw rocks through his windows and left dead rats in his postbox.

The lesson of Barry's life was not lost on young William. Those who supported the established views were rolling in riches, while those who challenged them were left poor and unemployed.

William's brush with the Academy was short-lived. Though he continued to exhibit his paintings there over the years, his rebel spirit could not endure the stifling atmosphere of the place for long.

As if to signal his liberation, William engraved a plate called *Glad Day*. It was purely for his own pleasure, and it provides a first glimpse of his own peculiar genius. Several years later, he enlarged and colored it. The design reveals a

Glad Day, *a design originally engraved by Blake in 1780.*

young male with arms spread wide in a gesture of freedom. He stands with one foot on the ground, as if in the act of springing from the earth. His hair flames out like fire, and his face is full of energy and determination.

It is said to be an illustration of the lines from *Romeo and Juliet*:

Night's candles are burnt out and jocund day
Stands tiptoe on the misty mountain tops.

And on one level, the almost luminous figure can be seen as a symbol of the rising sun, pushing back the darkness. But on another level, it is an image of William himself, rejoicing in the unfolding of his own vision, and casting off all that would restrain it.

As an engraver, William had been taught to weave an intricate web of lines over all his figures to give them depth and dimension. At the same time, it was as though he were binding those figures in a confining net. But here, in signaling his liberation from all systems, William freed the figure as well.

To bring in money, William continued to look for engraving commissions. His work brought him into contact with a number of other young artists who shared his ideals in art and with whom he formed lifelong friendships.

Thomas Stothard was two years older than William and a respected illustrator. He was gentle and quiet, but had an immense energy. At fifteen he had been apprenticed to a silk patternmaker. In his spare hours, his master had encouraged the boy to draw and paint. When the publisher of a magazine happened to see his work one day, he asked young Stothard if he would like to try his hand at illustrating for his magazine. Stothard completed a number of pieces on approval. They were accepted, and his course was set.

He was so prolific an artist that a host of journeymen engravers, William among them, were assigned the task of engraving from his designs. Stothard shared William's passion for the Gothic and, in particular, for the ancient tombs in Westminster Abbey. The two became close friends and would often meet in the evening to draw and paint.

Frequently another of Stothard's friends, John Flaxman, would join them. Flaxman was the son of a plaster-cast maker whose shop was in the Strand, not far from Blake's neighborhood near Golden Square. Having been raised among the plaster-casts and models that his father made and repaired, it is little wonder that, at an early age, the boy himself turned to sculpture. He was a delicate young man who suffered from a slight curvature of the spine. Still, he was to become one of the most influential English artists of the age. In 1781, Flaxman married and set up his home and studio very near Blake's home. They became good friends.

Blake was not an easy man. He had a sharp tongue and was quick to take offence. Later, there would be bitter quarrels with both these friends, but, for now, the waters ran smooth and the young artists drew support from one another.

At about this time, Blake began a friendship with another artist who was to prove very influential. Henry Fuseli, the son of a Swiss painter, was sixteen years older than Blake and was thirty-nine when he settled in Broad Street in 1780 and became a neighbor. He was famous and widely traveled.

There was a marked element of the fantastic in Fuseli's work that mirrored Blake's own tastes. They shared a strong dislike for drawing from life. One of Fuseli's most famous remarks, "Nature puts me out," could easily have come from the mouth of Blake.

Fuseli was an extravagant figure. He was barely five feet tall, and wore high top boots. As a result of a fever he had suffered during a stay in Italy, his hair had turned pure white. He kept it neatly powdered. His dress was elegant, his conversation striking – and liberally sprinkled with oaths.

He was a great wit. He later taught at the Royal Academy and was a favorite with his students. Inspecting a student's drawing one day, he quipped, "It is bad; take it into the fields and shoot it. That's a good boy." When someone remarked that the boat he had depicted in his painting *The Miracle of the Loaves and the Fishes* was too small, he replied without a pause, "That's part of the miracle."

It is likely that Blake and Fuseli first met through an engraving project, and the two men worked together on a number of projects over the next several years. Fuseli would later say of Blake that the time would come when the finest of his designs "would be as much sought after and treasured . . . as those of Michael Angelo now."

Riots were a fact of life in eighteenth-century London. Some were the spontaneous uprisings of the poor against threats to their livelihood or the sudden sharp rise in the price of bread. But others were orchestrated from above, by members of the ruling class who "raised a mob" for some political gain. The Gordon Riots, the most violent in London's history, were a case of the latter. And twenty-three-year-old William Blake was swept up in the tide of terror that surged through London's streets in June 1780 and was lucky to escape with his life.

England was then at war, not only with her rebellious American colonies but also with the Catholic powers of France and Spain. Protestant England had a longstanding anti-Catholic tradition. "Popery" was commonly associated with the threat of foreign enslavement. Lord George Gordon, the flamboyant twenty-nine-year-old son of the Duke of Gordon, was anti-Catholic to the core.

Certain recent government measures enraged him. The Catholic Relief Act of 1778, designed to remedy long-standing injustices against Catholics in England, was widely unpopular with the Protestant majority. The act gave Catholics the right to inherit and dispose of property, and Catholic priests the right to practise their vocation unmolested. It was the government's attempt to win favor with the large Catholic population in Scotland and Ireland, from which England hoped to enlist troops to fight in the war against her American colonies.

Lord Gordon was furious. He formed the Protestant Association and circulated a petition to Parliament to repeal the Relief Act. On June 2, 1780, he led close to five thousand supporters through the streets of London to the House of Commons, with the petition in hand. He had gathered forty-four thousand signatures.

The crowd started out sedately, but as they marched along they were joined by rowdy young men fired with drink who were upset with the influx of Irish Catholic workers competing for their jobs. When Parliament refused to bow to the pressure of the mob on its doorstep, and postponed debate on the issue, the largely peaceful demonstration quickly escalated into the most spectacular riot of the century.

For a week, the rioting went on unabated. City authorities, in sympathy with the mob, silently stood by while Catholic chapels, schools, and the businesses and homes of prominent Catholic supporters of the bill were pulled down and their contents burned in the streets.

On the first night of the rioting, the crowd surged along Broad Street on its way to torch and plunder the private chapel at the Bavarian Embassy in Golden Square. Fourteen rioters were arrested and five sent to Newgate Prison. The rioting continued over the next two nights, and now the crowd targeted the houses of those who had arrested and sentenced the rioters.

Newgate Prison, London's oldest and largest prison, had recently been rebuilt and was hailed as the strongest prison in England. But on June 6, the mob determined to march on Newgate to free their captured comrades. As the crowd stormed through the streets armed with bludgeons and crowbars, Blake, who happened to be out walking, was swept along with the angry mob and witnessed the events firsthand.

The mob stormed and burned the prison. The great gates soon fell before the assault of sledgehammers and crowbars. While the rioters scaled the walls and tore away the roof and rafters, the fire raged and the prisoners inside, in danger of being burned alive, shrieked and wailed. Many were hauled up through the roof, still in their chains, and rescued by the mob. In all, three hundred prisoners escaped. Soldiers, on being ordered to fire on the rioters and the released prisoners, laid down their arms.

On the following day, known as Black Wednesday, the rioting reached its peak. A large distillery, owned by a Catholic businessman, was broken into and set ablaze. More than 120,000 gallons of gin stored in the cellars were ignited.

Attack on Newgate Prison during the Gordon Riots.

Rioters lay in the gutter, scooping up the flaming liquor, while the fire raged out of control, destroying twenty-one neighboring houses.

It was not until the rioters threatened to storm the Bank of England itself that the government finally called in the military. There were heavy casualties. All told, over three hundred died and fifty buildings were destroyed. Lord Gordon was arrested and imprisoned in the Tower.

In chilling retribution, scores of rioters, many mere boys, were publicly hung. "I never heard boys cry so" was the comment of one bystander. Fortunately, William was not recognized by the military as one among the mob at Newgate Prison, or he might have suffered the same fate.

CHAPTER FOUR

JOY AND WOE

AIR

 OMETIME OVER THE NEXT YEAR, WILLIAM FELL HEAD OVER heels in love with a girl named Polly Wood. He began to court her. She seemed to return his affection, and soon he was planning to ask her to marry him. But Polly was not the marrying kind. In fact, William found out she was seeing another man behind his back. When he confronted her, she turned on him and asked scornfully, "Are you a fool?"

It broke William's heart. To mend it, he went to visit relatives in the pretty village of Battersea, across the river from London. During his stay, he lodged at the home of William Boucher, a market-gardener who grew vegetables for the London market. Boucher and his wife and their ten children managed to eke out a living on their land, but luxuries such as education were beyond their humble means. At ten years of age, the children either became servants, or worked the fields alongside their father. Their youngest child, Catherine, now nineteen, worked as a maid in one of the better houses in the neighborhood for bed and board, and came home on Sundays to spend time with her family.

One fine Sunday, the pretty, dark-eyed girl returned home to find young William Blake staying with the family. In later years, she said that as soon as she set eyes on him, she knew that this was the man she would marry. Faint with emotion, she fled the room. Later that night, while the two sat quietly talking in a corner, William told her the sad tale of Polly Wood. She responded with sympathy and understanding.

"Do you pity me, then?" he asked her.

She looked into his deep eyes and said, "Indeed I do."

"Then I love you for that," he replied.

"Well, and I love you."

With these few words, their future was set. William returned to his father's house in London and, over the following year, took on extra engraving commissions and worked hard to save enough money to marry.

On August 18, 1782, the couple were wed in Battersea Church. William signed his name in the parish register. Catherine made her mark with an *X*. He was twenty-five, she twenty. It was a match made in heaven. Never were two people more perfectly suited. For the next forty-five years, they were practically inseparable. They lived and worked together and supported one another through all the joys and sorrows of life.

The newlyweds moved to London, where they rented a flat in a house owned by a tailor at 23 Green Street, Leicester Fields. City and country came together in the neighborhood. At dawn the roosters crowed, and hens and chickens strutted along the streets. The young couple's favorite pastime was to take long walks into the countryside that William had so loved as a boy. They would walk out for twenty miles or more, stop at an inn for a bite to eat, then make the long trek home and think nothing of it.

*The young Blake,
at age twenty-eight,
from a pencil
drawing by
Catherine Blake.*

In their spare time, William taught Catherine to read and write and gave her lessons in drawing. She would often sit watching him while he worked. Gradually she learned the arts of engraving, painting, and printing so well that, in later years, she often worked with him.

Thanks mainly to the support of his friend Thomas Stothard, engraving commissions continued to come in. John Flaxman also tried to bring his friend to the notice of those who might assist him. He introduced William to the circle surrounding Mrs. Harriet Mathew, a gifted and elegant member of polite society. Along with her husband, Reverend Anthony Stephen Mathew, she was a patron to promising young artists. She had taken Flaxman under her wing while he was still a boy and encouraged him to study Greek. As thanks for her kindness, he decorated her library in the Gothic style, with sculpted figures of sand and putty set in niches in the wall, and furniture designed in imitation of the ancients.

Mrs. Mathew held regular gatherings at her house in Rathbone Place, attended by many of the literary and artistic community. Into this highly refined environment, Flaxman brought his fiery friend William Blake.

In addition to drawing and painting, William had been writing poetry since he was a boy. Some of it echoed the popular poetry of the day, some of it imitated the style of poets of a former age; but some of it struck a new note entirely his own. He must have shown his poems to Flaxman, who encouraged him to bring them to the attention of Mrs. Mathew and her influential friends.

And so, with his poems in hand, William entertained the Mathews' circle, sometimes reading the poems aloud, sometimes singing them to tunes he had composed himself. According to a friend who was there, "He was listened to by the company with profound silence, and allowed by most of the visitors to possess original and extraordinary merit."

Here is perhaps the most famous of those poems, said to have been composed before he was fourteen:

How sweet I roam'd from field to field,
    And tasted all the summer's pride,
'Till I the prince of love beheld,
    Who in the sunny beams did glide!

He shew'd me lilies for my hair,
    And blushing roses for my brow;
He led me through his gardens fair,
    Where all his golden pleasures grow.

With sweet May dews my wings were wet,
    And Phoebus fir'd my vocal rage;
He caught me in his silken net,
    And shut me in his golden cage.

He loves to sit and hear me sing,
    Then, laughing, sports and plays with me;
Then stretches out my golden wing,
    And mocks my loss of liberty.

All went well for a time. The Mathews admired the young poet's gifts, and he became a regular guest at their gatherings. Mrs. Mathew persuaded her husband to join Flaxman in supporting the cost of printing these early poems. The result was a slim pamphlet of seventy pages entitled *Poetical Sketches*, neither well printed nor well edited. It was accompanied by a preface by Reverend Mathew in which he apologizes for the "irregularities and defects" of the poems and hopes that their originality might merit them "some respite from oblivion." The author of the poems is identified only as W.B.

Blake was presented with the uncorrected, unbound sheets. Some he assembled, corrected halfheartedly by hand, and gave to friends and acquaintances; but, in fact, he showed little interest in the entire affair.

Despite his efforts, it seemed he was as doomed here as in the halls of the Royal Academy, to be looked on as an "untutored youth" with aspirations beyond his station. Yes, he had talent, they seemed to say, but as for these pretensions to being a poet or a painter, it was really quite absurd. An engraver he was, and an engraver he would stay.

William continued to attend the Mathews' gatherings for a time, but it soon became clear that he simply did not fit in. When provoked, he could be wild and outrageous in his way of speaking. His opinions, according to one who was there, were "not at all times considered pleasing by everyone," and soon "his visits were not so frequent." There was clearly a collision between the passionate young poet and the rigidly class-conscious society in which he found himself. Years later, he was to write

> The Enquiry in England is not whether a man has Talents & Genius, But whether he is Passive & Polite & a Virtuous Ass & obedient to Noblemen's Opinions in Art & Science. If he is, he is a Good Man. If Not, he must be Starved.

In the summer of 1784, William's father died and was buried in the Dissenters' Burying Ground at Bunhill Fields. William's older brother James took over the family business. William had been getting by, but certainly not prospering, with his commissioned engravings for the book and magazine trade. It troubled him deeply that he seemed destined to waste his talents in mere mechanical copying of another's designs, particularly when it seemed that the inspiration for those designs had at times been borrowed from his own work.

In a bid for independence, he started a print-selling business with fellow apprentice and now friend from the Basire days, James Parker. Parker was a mild-mannered, conscientious man. He and his wife, Anne, took a house together with William and Catharine at 27 Broad Street, next to the Blake family home, and set up shop.

"A Print shop was a rare bird in London" at the time, Blake later recalled. However, the market for commercial prints to decorate the walls of houses was growing, and the business required little money beyond the purchase of a stock of prints and a place to sell them from.

As trained engravers, Blake and Parker would be able to engrave prints for sale in their shop. If they could print those engravings themselves, another expense would be eliminated. And so, with money he had likely inherited from his father, William purchased for forty pounds the wooden rolling press that was to accompany him the rest of his life.

A wooden rolling press similar to that owned by Blake.

Most London businesses at the time were open from six in the morning until nine at night. Catherine regularly worked the showroom at the front of the shop. She was a good saleswoman, careful not to show her customers too many things at once. Blake and Parker spent most of their time in the studio behind the showroom, engraving and pulling prints.

Despite their best efforts, business was slow and profits were small. The men were forced to continue their regular commissioned work for other print-publishers, and probably added the twenty free proofs they received for each job to the stock of prints for sale at the shop.

After little more than a year, the pressure of two families sharing cramped quarters under strained circumstances proved too much. They decided to part company. Parker kept the stock of prints and continued in the print-selling business. William and Catherine kept the press and moved to 28 Poland Street, three streets away, where they lived for the next five years.

William's brother Robert came to live with them there. Though Robert was five years younger, a close bond existed between the brothers. William taught Robert to draw, paint, and engrave. He drew figures for Robert to copy in his notebook and suggested subjects for him to work on. Teaching suited William, and he turned to it repeatedly over the years. The brothers worked side by side, bending over each other's work and offering praise and encouragement.

It was a happy time. William had begun to collect some of the poems he had already written and to compose new ones, with the idea of bringing them together in a book of verse for children. He wasn't the first to have the idea. Isaac Watts had published his *Divine Songs for the Use of Children* in 1715. The book had been immensely popular and spawned a host of imitations. These and the many books in prose now being written for children were intended to show them their duty to God and man.

But the poems William had begun to write were shockingly different. They spoke with the voice of the child itself, and were celebrations of the joy and freedom of childhood. Far from instructing children in adult ways, they attempted to capture the child's vision.

William had little hope of finding a commercial publisher for such a book. It was simply too different. And so, as he talked it over with Robert, he decided that he must find a way of publishing that would be in keeping with the spirit of the poems themselves. Perhaps he could print the book himself. After all, he had his own press.

He toyed with the idea of using his skills to engrave the poems on copper plates, accompanying each with a "high finished print." But such a method would be slow and tedious. The text would all have to be engraved in reverse, so that it would read right when printed. And to engrave so many illustrations

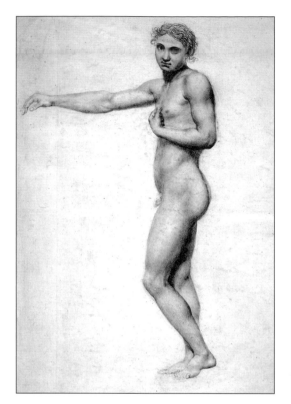

An early study by Blake, possibly of his brother Robert, c. 1779.

would be just as tedious. Engraving was his trade, but he had come to realize that, in many ways, it was also his prison.

These poems were celebrations of freedom, remembrances of his own visionary childhood. He wanted a simple and spontaneous way of reproducing them that would allow him the same freedom he found in drawing sketches for Robert to copy. He imagined being able to draw and write directly on the copper as if it were a canvas, creating an image he could print and reproduce. But how? He continued to discuss the idea with Robert and Catherine, but the secret eluded him.

Often on a Sunday, the three of them would walk together in the country-side, visiting Catherine's family in Battersea and rediscovering William's boyhood haunts in the Surrey hills.

Still, things did not always run smoothly in the small house. One day Catherine and Robert got into a quarrel. In the heat of the moment, she spoke sharply to him. Immediately William sprang up. "Kneel down and beg Robert's pardon directly," he demanded, "or you will never see my face again."

Though she found it difficult to beg for forgiveness when she did not feel herself at fault, Catherine knelt down and murmured, "Robert, I beg your pardon. I am in the wrong."

"Young woman, you lie," said Robert. "I am in the wrong." And so, with a few selfless words, all was forgiven.

But tragedy soon befell the little household. Robert became ill. He lost weight, grew pale, and was wracked by violent fits of coughing. Sometimes he coughed up blood. All of these were the grim symptoms of tuberculosis, and there was no cure.

By early 1787, he was bedridden. The disease soon reached a crisis point, and it was clear that Robert was going to die. For two weeks William sat at his brother's bedside day and night, refusing to rest. After a long and bitter struggle, Robert died. At the moment of his passing, William had a vision of his brother's spirit ascending through the ceiling, "clapping its hands for joy." He took to his bed and slept for three days and three nights without waking.

In the dark months following Robert's death, William found spiritual solace in the writings of Emanuel Swedenborg. It was probably John Flaxman who introduced his friend to the work of the Swedish seer, for Flaxman was himself a devoted follower.

Emanuel Swedenborg was a famous scientist, who, at fifty-six, underwent a spiritual experience that transformed his life. He turned his back on science and, for the rest of his long life, devoted himself to exploring the spirit world and recording what he saw there.

Like Blake, he was a visionary. His visions came at night, on the borderland between waking and sleep. In this state, he claimed that the spirit world had opened to him, and he was able to speak with the spirits who inhabited that world.

Swedenborg felt that death was only the doorway to a new life, that when we shed our physical bodies, we stand in our spiritual ones and live on in the spiritual world. He believed that the material world sprang from and was a reflection of that inner world and that everything in nature was a symbol of some spiritual reality. He called these symbols *correspondences*. He said that the ancients had understood this spiritual language of correspondence, that the biblical prophets spoke it in their prophesies, but that the understanding of it had long been lost. He claimed to have found the key.

To a poet like Blake, this was profoundly inspiring. Not only did it support his own experience of vision, but it also gave him hope that even though his dear Robert was gone from this world, he lived on in another with which William could communicate. For a time, he embraced Swedenborg's doctrines wholeheartedly. He bought and annotated copies of the writer's works, and he and Catherine attended the founding meeting of the Swedenborgian New Jerusalem Church at a London pub in April 1789.

However, Blake soon came to have grave doubts about much of Swedenborg's teaching. He was troubled by the rigid system of rewards and punishments that structured Swedenborg's vision of the spiritual world and by his attempt to explain rationally what lay beyond the reach of reason. Still, the Swedish seer's influence upon William and his work was enduring.

With Robert's death, a door had opened for Blake between the inner world of spirit and vision and the outer world. Communication between these two worlds would now become a distinguishing feature of his beliefs, the source of much of his inspiration, and the mark of what others saw as his eccentricity. In a letter to the poet William Hayley in 1800, he wrote

Thirteen years ago I lost a brother & with his spirit I converse daily & hourly in the Spirit, & See him in my remembrance in the regions of my Imagination. I hear his advice & even now write from his Dictate.

Throughout his life, William kept his brother's notebook by his side as a sign of his spiritual presence. Here he wrote the drafts of many of his most famous poems, and to its pages he committed his most private thoughts. Alongside his brother's sketches in the book, he roughed out his own. It was here, shortly after Robert's death, that he drew the series of mysterious pictures that would evolve into the little emblem book he called *The Gates of Paradise.*

CHAPTER FIVE

THE DISCOVERY

FIRE

HE ST. JAMES WORKHOUSE STOOD ON THE GROUNDS OF AN old cemetery known as Pawlett's Garden, which lay almost directly behind the Blake family home on Broad Street. For a number of years William's father supplied stockings and caps to the workhouse, and it is possible that, as a boy, William made deliveries and met some of the children who lived there.

The plight of workhouse children in London was a longstanding scandal. Orphaned, abandoned, or given up by parents too poor to raise them, these children were at the mercy of often cruel nurses and unscrupulous parish officers who were paid a one-time lump sum for the children in their care, and who stood to profit from their speedy deaths. After 1762, parishes were required by law to keep a record of their "infant poor." These showed that of one hundred infants under one year of age in the care of the parishes, only seven survived until the age of three.

In response to these shocking statistics, an Act of Parliament was passed in 1767 requiring all parish children to be sent outside London to the care of nurses in the country. Independently, St. James parish had launched such a program five years earlier. They made arrangements with several cottagers in Wimbledon Common, just the other side of the river, to board parish children for three shillings a week per child. A cottager caring for five or six children could earn a decent income. A doctor was assigned to oversee the children's care.

Children stayed in this rural setting until they were six or seven years old. The older ones were sent to school and taught to read and sew. To prevent them from being returned to the vice and disease rampant in the workhouse itself, a school was established in 1782 a short distance away. It was known as the school of industry or, more commonly, the house in King Street. Children returning from the country were boarded and educated there from the ages of seven to fourteen, when most of them became apprentices.

There is no parallel for the care St. James parish took of its poor children. Such an extensive education for the children of the poor was unheard of before this. By 1783, there were one hundred boys and one hundred girls living at the King Street school. While at the workhouse, the death rate among children was alarmingly high, in the first fifteen years of its operation, only six children died at the new school.

※

In the happy days when Robert was still alive and the three of them would take long walks in the country, the Blakes likely witnessed firsthand the experiment with the workhouse children. Wimbledon Common, where the children were boarded, was just two miles from Battersea, where Catherine's parents lived. The sight of these rescued children may well have inspired the poems William was writing at the time.

During the dark months after his brother's death, he jotted down drafts of new poems on the blank pages at the back of Robert's notebook, even as he continued sketching the series of small drawings at the front. Some would later be used to illustrate the new poems. As he worked, William mulled over the ideas the two of them had often discussed about a new way of printing. But still his thoughts ran up against walls.

Then, one night as he slept, Robert's spirit appeared to him in a vision and revealed the answer he had been seeking for so long. First thing the next morning, he and Catherine gathered together what money they had. She hurried off and bought the simple materials they would need to set the process in motion – pitch, turpentine, and linseed oil.

Blake blended the pitch and the linseed oil to make a thick liquid. He then diluted it with turpentine until it was thin enough to flow freely from his brush and quill pen. This simple mixture was the key. With it, he could write and draw directly onto a copper plate. He needed to work fast, for the liquid dried quickly. And once it dried, it formed a hard varnishlike coating on the plate.

He began experimenting. He chose one of Robert's designs, *The Approach of Doom*, copying it onto the plate in quick fluid motions, in the same way he would have copied it onto paper. Then, around the edges of the plate, he formed a wax wall and carefully poured a solution of nitric acid onto the plate to a depth of about a quarter of an inch.

As it reacted with the metal, the acid became hot, turned blue, and began to bite into the copper. It bubbled about the edge of the design he had drawn on the plate, but could not bite away the varnish. Slowly, over several hours, the acid burned away the unvarnished parts of the plate to a depth of about a sixteenth of an inch, leaving the design he had drawn standing in relief upon it.

It was now a relatively simple matter to clean the plate, ink the design carefully so as not to allow the ink to touch any other part, then pass the plate through his press with a sheet of damp paper laid on it to take the image.

Like many discoveries, it had taken a known technique and turned it on its head. Both the varnish William had used to draw with and the acid were

Fragment of a plate from the poem America: A Prophecy, 1793. *The only surviving example of Blake's original relief etched plates. Note how the image and text stand raised above the surface of the plate.*

materials common to engravers. As an apprentice, he had been taught the art of etching along with engraving. To etch a design into a plate, you first covered the plate with a ground of wax or varnish. Using an etching needle, you cut your design through that ground, exposing the metal underneath. You then poured acid over the plate, which bit into the exposed portions but was repelled by the wax or varnish. But here, instead of using the acid in the usual way to strengthen the lines of a design on the plate, and the varnish to repel the acid from other areas, William had done exactly the opposite. Instead of biting his design into the plate with the acid, he used the acid to burn away everything but the design.

And so, from a vision in the night that led to the discovery of a simple technique using simple materials, much of the work for which we remember William Blake flowed.

Over the next few months, William and Catherine continued to experiment with the new process, which he called Illuminated Printing. In addition to Robert's *The Approach of Doom*, William produced several other small designs, composing directly on the copper.

He soon took his first tentative steps toward marrying the arts of writing and painting on the printed page. In order for the words to read right, William had to write them on the plate in reverse, a skill he had learned as an engraver. He put that skill to use as he composed *There is No Natural Religion* and *All Religions Are One*. The pages are small, roughly 2¼" × 1½". The drawings are deliberately simple, the words are few. But within their narrow boundaries we find the first expression of Blake's visionary beliefs.

He who sees the infinite in all things sees God.
He who sees the Ratio only, sees himself only.

William never published these first minute pieces. Instead they served as the workshop for experimenting with the new technique, determining the proper

Songs of Innocence, *title page, 1789.*
(Please see front endpapers for color
reproduction of this image.)

inking, the proper pressures, but, above all, planting the visionary seeds that were soon to blossom into the splendor of *Songs of Innocence.*

In *Songs of Innocence*, William realized the dream of publishing a book of poems for children entirely by his own hand. He was free from publishers and their demands for books that fit the taste of the times, free from condescending patrons. He was free to weave all his talents together into one harmonious whole.

These songs, the first fruits of Blake's new method of uniting the arts of painting and poetry, are themselves celebrations of a world of unity and harmony. The poems, some dating back to his days with the Mathews, speak in a variety of voices, young and old, but what unites them is the vision of joy and peace they share. Each poem is like a little window onto a portion of paradise.

The boundaries between one creature and another have fallen away; the walls between inside and outside have dissolved. It is springtime, and the sun that calls the blossom from its bed brings all living things to bloom. Children bloom with joy; the very words on the page leaf out, flame, and flower with the one life that opens in and through all things, great and small.

The poems are not simply words printed on a page. The words are swept up in the designs that surround them, so that the designs that illuminate the poem are part of the poem, and both are expressions of the joyful vision of life that pulses through them.

In one of these poems, "Nurse's Song," Blake shows us the world of Innocence. The poem opens with the words

When the voices of children are heard on the green
And laughing is heard on the hill,
My heart is at rest within my breast
And everything else is still.

It is the nurse who speaks the poem. The children of the poem are in her care, as the workhouse children were cared for by their nurses on Wimbledon Common. Innocence reigns where all are cared for and kept from harm. Indeed the nurse in the poem is as much in the care of the children as they are in hers, for their joy brings her peace and rest.

In the design that accompanies the poem, the nurse is pictured reading a book. Could it be this very poem she is reading? Notice the human figures frolicking among the letters of the title and in the foliage beneath. Below, the children, linked hand in hand, play "In and out the Window," as the readers go in and out the window of this poem.

The sun is sinking and the dark draws near, but the children do not wish to

"Nurse's Song" from Songs
of Innocence.

stop playing. In fact, their play appears to hold the night at bay, as the birds fly through the sky and the sheep graze upon the hills, which echo back the children's laughter. It is only the reader who stands at the window, who feels the full weight of the fading of the light that must surely follow.

Working together, William and Catherine printed sixteen copies of *Songs of Innocence.* The book contained thirty-one plates. Each copy was colored by hand and stitched in paper wrappers. As these copies sold, new copies were printed over the years. For all its beauty, most of Blake's contemporaries considered *Songs* to be crudely produced and primitive in appearance. Though it is still the book Blake is best known for, and the one he printed most copies of in his lifetime, the total number of separate known copies is only twenty-five.

In *The Book of Thel*, his next Illuminated Book, Blake took as his theme the fading of the light foreshadowed in "Nurse's Song." The poem consists of seven delicately colored plates and is, in many respects, the most beautiful of his early books. The heroine, Thel, is a figure who dwells on the boundary between two worlds. Though she still sees with the visionary eyes of Innocence, she is no longer one with that world. Something has happened. She has come face-to-face with the reality of death, and she is afraid. She laments:

> O life of this our spring! why fades the lotus of the water,
> Why fade these children of the spring, born but to smile and fall?
> Ah! Thel is like a wat'ry bow, and like a parting cloud;
> Like a reflection in a glass; like shadows in the water . . .

She is addressed in turn by a Lily of the valley, a Cloud, and a Clod of Clay, each of which reveal to her their human form and attempt to teach her the humble wisdom that "Everything that lives lives not alone nor for itself." In the act of selfless love, one fulfills one's purpose in life and need have no fear of death. For "he that loves the lowly" will keep each in his care.

The Clod of Clay invites Thel to enter her house and see "the secrets of the land unknown."

> Wilt thou, O Queen, enter my house? 'Tis given thee to enter
> And to return: fear nothing.

Thel enters and finds herself wandering through "a land of sorrows and of tears." She comes to her own grave plot, but at the sounds of sorrow breathing from the pit, she flees in fear. Unable to pass through the death of self into a

Thel, "the matron Clay," and the infant Worm, from The Book of Thel, *1789.*

fuller life, Thel flees back "unhinder'd till she came into the vales of Har." With that, the poem ends.

The Book of Thel takes place on the boundary between Innocence and Experience. The Lily of the valley, the Cloud, and the Clod of Clay show Thel how to carry the wisdom of Innocence beyond that boundary. Fleeing it, Thel enters the somber land that will form the setting for the dark companion piece to *Songs of Innocence* – the *Songs of Experience*.

With Robert's death, William had come into that dark country where Death seems to rule. *Songs of Innocence* had been a memorial to those blissful days before Death had entered their world. But even as he worked toward publishing these poems, he was writing others of a darker nature. After Robert died, William realized the joyful poems of *Songs of Innocence* had to be paired with poems that reflect the contrary state of the human soul. Not only is joy to be found in the world; a dark thread of sorrow runs through all things as well. Were all life's joys fated to end in sorrow? Was Evil destined to prosper in the world and Good to suffer? William had found comfort in Swedenborg before, but for the questions that troubled him now, no answers appeared in Swedenborg's system. It was not a system he needed, but a vision.

He was to find that vision in the writings of a man who had himself struggled with the same questions, a man in many ways like him – the German shoemaker visionary Jacob Boehme.

⁂

Jacob Boehme was born in 1575 in a small market town near the city of Görlitz, Germany. His parents were simple pious folk. At fourteen, he was apprenticed to a shoemaker, and in that trade he would make his living. He married and settled in Görlitz with his family. Then, at twenty-five, he had a vision that transformed his life.

He was studying his Bible one day, searching for answers to the sorrows that troubled him, when he glanced up and saw the sunlight reflected off a polished pewter dish. Suddenly he felt himself filled with the light of God. He went outside, and it seemed to him that in and through all things, even in the herbs and grasses of the field, he saw God.

The vision faded. In the ten long years that followed, he studied and meditated upon it, and finally wrote down the fruits of his meditations in a book, meant only as a memorial for himself. He called the book *Aurora*.

He wrote the book early in the morning, before opening his shop. The words tumbled out. "Art has not written this," he wrote, "but all was ordered according to the direction of the Spirit . . . it goes and comes like a sudden shower."

He loaned his book to a friend, who had it copied without his knowledge. A copy came into the hands of the pastor of the church in Görlitz, who denounced the mild shoemaker from the pulpit and threatened to have him banished if he did not stop writing. Boehme laid aside his pen for five years. Then, at the urging of friends, and with the conviction that he must put his talent to use "and not return to God single and without improvement like a lazy servant," he began to write again.

For the next six years he wrote book after book, until a copy of one of his works fell into the pastor's hands again. In 1623, he was banished from his town and his family. He was taken in by friends, and his fame spread. The next year, he fell ill and returned home to die.

On the night he died, he told those gathered around that he heard beautiful music and asked that they open the door so that he might better hear it. Then, calling his family to his side to bid them farewell, with a smile on his face, he spoke his final words: "Now I go to Paradise."

At the heart of Boehme's vast and often chaotic work lie two basic insights, both of which Blake embraced. The first is that *the All is in the small.* The world and all that live in it are a manifestation of God. The whole being of God is present in everything that lives.

Therefore, we need not go far to find God. We need only look into ourselves. And finding God there, we see the same God shining in and through all things. This vision is echoed in Blake's famous lines from "Auguries of Innocence":

To see a World in a Grain of Sand
And a Heaven in a Wild Flower,
Hold Infinity in the palm of your hand
And Eternity in an hour.

But we do not live steadily in the light of this vision. It comes and it goes. It opens and it closes. In all things there is light and darkness, joy and sorrow, peace and strife, unity and division. It is this experience that lies at the root of Boehme's second insight, that *in Yes and No all things consist.*

Were this not so, nothing would exist. There would be only a vast stillness. Two kingdoms strive within us, one of darkness and one of light, and toward which of them we tend, in that we live. The kingdom of darkness is the part of us that seeks to enclose us, that surrounds us like a shell, constrains us like a cocoon. Boehme calls it Selfhood. Its light is reason; its rule is law. It denies vision and delights in power.

Constantly opposed to it is the kingdom of light – the part of us that strives to open, to expand its wings, to break through the shell that constrains it and fly free. As that world opens in us, we see the same world opening in all that lives and are at one with them. This condition of harmony and freedom, where each creature strives to bring the life that opens in it to bloom, is what Blake celebrated in his *Songs of Innocence.*

⁂

The first translations of Boehme's work into English, a hundred years before Blake was born, influenced the early Dissenters, the religious tradition into which William was born. Now, in the wake of Robert's death, he returned to those roots.

We learn to see ourselves in the mirror of other lives. In the life of Jacob Boehme, Blake found a mirror in which to see himself.

CHAPTER SIX

LAMBETH: THE FIGURE ON THE STAIRS

AT LENGTH FOR HATCHING
RIPE HE BREAKS THE SHELL

N THE FALL OF 1790, WILLIAM AND CATHERINE LEFT THE neighborhood of his family home and moved across the Thames to Lambeth, in Surrey. Lambeth was just beginning to be developed. Rows of houses were built alongside country roads and lanes that ran through meadows and marshland.

Number 13 Hercules Building was one such house. The street may have taken its name from one of the performers in the circus operated by Philip Astley, who had developed the area and lived just two doors away. The circus, too, was in the neighborhood, as well as the Bethlehem Asylum for Lunatics, the Female Orphan Asylum, and Lambeth Palace, residence of the Archbishop of Canterbury.

Hercules Buildings, Lambeth, the Blakes' home from 1790 to 1800. It is here that Blake produced many of his best-known works, among them The Gates of Paradise.

Number 13 was a pretty house of eight or ten rooms on three floors. The front faced north and looked across open fields to the river. Out back was a long strip of garden bordered by poplars.

The Blakes had never had the luxury of a garden before. They planted a fig tree and built an arbor, training a grape vine up its side until soon it was a shady nook luxuriant with leaves, where they would sit and drink their tea and read together.

One day, as he was coming in from the garden, William had the fright of his life. He glanced up the staircase that led from the garden door into the house and saw a terrifying figure, all "scaly, speckled, and very awful," coming down the stairs toward him. He had seen many visions in his life, but never such a horrible specter. He turned and ran from the house.

Perhaps the grim figure on the staircase hailed from the dark world that occupied Blake's mind so much at this time. For now he was busy putting together the poems that would depict the contrary state to the joyful vision of *Songs of Innocence.*

Everywhere he looked, he saw the darkening vision. The Surrey countryside he had so loved as a child, and which likely drew him to move to Lambeth now, was changing. Gone were the children sent from St. James Workhouse to thrive on Wimbledon Common. The enlightened program that had sent them there ended abruptly three years before, in the very year that Robert had died. The governors of the parish had decided that the expense of educating poor children beyond their station in life could no longer be justified. From then on, a deathly chill fell over their charity.

The children were made to work to earn their keep now. The house in King Street was transformed into a true school of industry. The girls were put to work sewing shirts and shifts and tablecloths. The boys were trained in mending shoes, cleaning cotton, and heading pins.

In 1790, the year the Blakes moved to Lambeth, plans were set in motion to mechanize the workhouse and put the poor to work. A factory was built over the burial ground at the back, ninety looms were installed, along with all the necessary machinery for a spinning and weaving operation.

A harsh new reality was abroad in the land. The age of the machine had dawned, and the poor and the powerless were enlisted in its service.

※

The roots of the new age reached back to the English Revolution of 1688. In its wake, Parliament won power over the king. The rich landowners who ruled

Parliament now, in effect, ruled the country, and set about increasing their wealth and power. Applying new scientific principles to farming their estates, they increased the size of their cattle and the yield of their crops.

They began to enclose their lands with fences, walls, and hedges. Small village farmers, who for centuries had worked the open fields and shared common land for grazing, found themselves suddenly dispossessed as they and their primitive methods stood in the landowners' way. Many flooded into London in hope of finding work; some stayed on as tenant farmers on the landowners' estates; still others took to spinning and weaving in their cottages for the cloth merchants in town.

England ruled a vast colonial empire. Woolen cloth was the staple export of the country, and the market for it was inexhaustible. The manufacturers could easily sell much more if only they had a way to produce it. Similar markets existed for cotton cloth, if only it could be spun and woven more efficiently.

And so a handful of wealthy entrepreneurs applied the same scientific principles to the textile industry that the landowners had applied to their farming. They called it the *rationalization* of industry, and it led directly to the industrial revolution.

Up until then, spinning and weaving had been a cottage industry. Weavers generally rented their looms from the merchants who bought their product. The work was a family affair and fell into the slow rhythms of rural life. The cotton was picked clean by the younger children, spun by the wife and daughters, and woven by the husband assisted by the sons. The weavers took pride in their craft, but worked only as much as necessary to get by. The rest of the time, they tended their animals and their gardens, and celebrated their traditions. In the name of rationalization, this way of life was destroyed.

In 1769 Richard Arkwright patented the water frame, a water-powered machine that could spin many threads at one time with mechanical fingers. He gathered many such machines together in one place, which he called a mill and we now call a factory. And he hired "hands" to operate those machines. By the 1780s, the steam engine, originally developed to pump water from the shafts of

A Weaver's Workshop. *Prior to the industrial revolution, weaving was a family affair, done in the weaver's home.*

coal mines, was put to use to turn the factory wheels. The country went "steam mill mad," and soon machines were not only spinning cotton and wool, but weaving them on power looms.

At the same time, new processes simplified the smelting of iron ore. Large blast furnaces appeared on the landscape. Molten iron was cast into molds and used in the construction of bridges, buildings, and larger, more powerful machines.

The machine was a thankless master. The steam engine was its iron heart; the blast furnace its fiery throat. It wrapped itself in a whirlwind of noise and smoke, and its power was without equal. The machine never grew weary, never rested, was blind to the sufferings of those who served it. According to a contemporary observer, "While the engine works, the people must work. Men, women and children are then yolk-fellows with iron and steam."

Factories sprang up all through the northern counties of England, close to the ready sources of coal that fed the machines. Grim factory towns grew around them, blackened by the soot that spewed from the factory chimneys. Workers lived short, desperate lives in ramshackle hovels, where whole families were crowded into single rooms. With drinking water fouled by factory pollutants, and garbage and sewage rotting in the streets, disease ran rampant and Death was a constant companion. The average life expectancy was eighteen, and over half the children died before the age of five.

In 1789 the governors of St. James Workhouse decided to start shipping children north as apprentices to a factory in Manchester. It was a way of relieving overcrowding and ridding themselves of the weaker and younger children, many of them girls difficult to place in other situations.

The factories required a steady supply of children to tend the machines. They were shipped by the cartload from the teeming workhouses of London, with little knowledge of the horrific situations into which they were being sent. And when they died, there were always more to take their place.

The factory owners employed mainly women and children to serve the machines. They were easier to control and cheaper to hire than men. Well over half the workers in the cotton mills were children, many as young as five. They worked sixteen-hour days, during which they commonly walked more than twenty miles among the machines. The doors were locked and the windows sealed, and temperatures on the factory floor often topped 80°F. The noise of the machines was so deafening that the workers developed a system of lipreading to communicate.

Foremen moved among the machines, armed with leather belts to beat those they found slacking or asleep from exhaustion. Safety regulations were

Working in a spinning mill.

nonexistent, and accidents were common. The father of a boy killed at a machine lamented, "If they will invent machines to supersede manual labour, they must find iron boys to mind them."

Throughout all this, the government stood wholly behind the "cotton lords" and their interests. Business was above regulation. The only regulations passed were against the workers, to prevent them from organizing to demand better conditions.

The chimneys of the industrial towns belched thick clouds of black smoke, which could be seen from miles away. The soot settled over the towns and over the lives of the lost souls who labored there.

How much Blake knew about the conditions in the north is uncertain, but even the pleasant countryside of Lambeth and Surrey offered no escape from the bleak realities of the new age. At every turn, he was met with reminders. Just a short distance north of their house in Hercules Buildings stood the first great modern factory in London. Designed by John Rennie, the Albion Flour Mill boasted cast-iron machinery rather than wood, and was able to produce close to six thousand bushels of flour a week. It was Rennie's attempt to show Londoners the marvels of the machine age and to open the way for further mechanization.

The building attracted a steady stream of sightseers, eager to view the new wonder. But there were also angry protesters, men put out of work by the machines. And in 1791, less than a year after Blake had moved into the area, the building was gutted by a mysterious fire and reduced to a blackened shell.

William and Catherine continued taking long walks into the Surrey countryside, but now, in addition to the familiar sights and sounds of the natural world, there were heralds of the new age. Along the banks of the Wandle River, several textile mills had been built. Soon a huge iron foundry took its place among them. War was in the wind. The foundry cast shot, shells, cannons, and other weapons. The roar of its blast furnace and the booming of its six-hundred-pound hammer filled the air.

It was not long before they would enter Blake's poetry as well, as in this passage from his poem *Milton*:

The Surrey hills glow like the clinkers of the furnace. . . .
Dark gleams before the Furnace-mouth a heap of burning ashes. . . .
Loud sounds the Hammer . . . loud turn the wheels. . . .

Iron Works for Casting Cannon, *Severn Gorge at Coalbrookdale. A scene similar to what Blake would have seen along the Wandle River in Surrey.*

Los lifts his iron Ladles
With molten ore; he heaves the iron cliffs in his rattling chains.

In 1789, the French peasants rose up and overthrew their rulers in a bloody revolution. The fever soon spread to England. Democratic clubs and societies sprang up, convinced that revolution in France was merely the first step in the liberation of all peoples. Blake was swept up in the general fervor, for it offered hope to all those who had suffered at the hands of wealth and power.

For some years, the bookseller Joseph Johnson had been the source of most of William's engraving commissions. Johnson's shop in St. Paul's Churchyard was the hub of a circle of writers and artists with radical views, among them Mary Wollstonecraft, William Godwin, and Thomas Paine.

*Joseph Johnson, radical
bookseller and Blake's
chief employer in the
1780s and '90s.*

Paine's book *The Rights of Man*, published in 1791, preached the gospel of revolution in plain language to the common people. He laid out a plan for education, relief of the poor, pensions for the aged, and public works for the unemployed. The authorities looked on all this with concern. Within a year, the publisher of the book was imprisoned, a ban was laid on future publication, and Paine was forced to flee England for France.

Part of the reason for repressive workhouse measures was the mounting fear that the poor would revolt. The government widely distributed cheap pamphlets aimed at teaching the poor respect for authority and "submission to poverty." The schools of industry were to keep the "inferior children" content with "the very lowest occupations in life."

The government instituted a program of intimidation to root out revolutionaries. People were pressured to declare loyalty to the Crown and to name those suspected of holding revolutionary views. Radicals, such as Johnson and his circle, were under increasing suspicion.

In this tense climate, Blake made his final attempt to publish his poetry in the traditional manner. The first book of a projected seven-book poem entitled *The French Revolution* was printed for Johnson, but it was never published. Did Johnson abandon the project as too dangerous, or did Blake change his mind?

Blake stood in sympathy with the radicals in their revolt against the tyranny of state religion and the rule of kings, in their opposition to slavery and the oppression of the poor. Yet he parted company with them in their belief in the supremacy of reason and their rejection of religion as a "tye to all able minds." It was always his view that the gospel preached by Jesus was "a perfect law of Liberty," that to reject state religion and enshrine reason was simply to replace one form of tyranny with another. And though, for a time, he supported the radicals – going so far as to wear the red cap of liberty openly in the street – once the French Revolution degenerated into the Reign of Terror, he removed the cap and distanced himself from the radical cause.

In the end, Blake was the champion not of reason, but of imagination. His concern was not with large movements but with the little people whose lives bob in the wake of all movements. He was a poet and an artist and a craftsman. And he turned all the strength of his imagination to one thing he felt could speak against the tyrannies of state and machine – the Illuminated Book.

CHAPTER SEVEN

"IN TIME OF TROUBLE"

ALAS!

 ILLIAM BLAKE WAS ONE OF THE FIRST ARTISTS TO RECOGNIZE the profound impact the machine age would have on art. Everywhere, he saw human values being replaced by mechanical values. Factories had changed the nature of work. The division of labor led to each person becoming responsible for a portion of a task, a portion that had in itself no real meaning. Hours were long, pay was poor, and workers became slaves to the machine.

Soon these same systems were applied to the production of art, turning "that which is Soul and Life into a Mill or Machine." As an engraver, William was in a unique position to view these changes. Even before the industrial revolution, many engraving studios had embraced a factory-like model of production. In the larger studios, one person might create the design, another etch the outline, and still others do various aspects of the finishing work. In fact, when the creators of the early factories were looking for a model of the division of labor, they found it in the large engraving studios.

But now, these modern systems of production were transforming the art of engraving itself. Art factories sprang up, where paintings were mass-produced as engravings in an assembly-line setting. Famous painters, such as Sir Joshua Reynolds, had stables of engravers working for them whose sole task was to reproduce paintings as engraved prints for the marketplace. More and more, the artist was being looked on as a manufacturer, the work of art a product, the aim profit.

Blake rebelled against all of this. Art for him was life, the life of the imagination. In the age of the machine, he believed that the duty of the artist was to safeguard the imagination, to keep "the Divine Vision in time of trouble." In an age flowing increasingly in the direction of fragmentation, he held up art as that which pointed to the unity of things.

But Blake was not merely an artist, he was a craftsman; he earned his money by the skilled work of his hands. Craftsmanship, too, was being threatened by the machine. As an artist and craftsman, he rejected the ways of the new age and adopted a purposely primitive form of production. For only by doing so was he able to exercise his talents freely and guard his unique gifts. His ideals were those of an earlier age. He dreamt of uniting the arts of writing and painting in the way the artists of the Middle Ages had united those arts in their illuminated manuscripts.

In *Songs of Innocence*, Blake had celebrated the joys of a visionary world of wholeness and harmony. But there was another, darker world constantly at war with that. In his own life, he had experienced the tyrannies of that world and had seen its mark stamped upon the lives of the poor and the powerless around him. It was to the depiction of that dark realm that he now turned the force of his pen in *Songs of Experience*. In the poem "Holy Thursday," he writes

> Is this a holy thing to see
> In a rich and fruitful land,
> Babes reduced to misery,
> Fed with cold and usurous hand?
>
> Is that trembling cry a song?
> Can it be a song of joy?
> And so many children poor?
> It is a land of poverty.

Songs of Experience are poems of oppression, control, and tyranny. The characters are "bound and weary," "chained in night." Many of the poems contrast with those in the first collection. For instance, "The Lamb" of *Innocence* is counterbalanced by "The Tyger" of *Experience*.

> Tyger, Tyger, burning bright
> In the forests of the night,
> What immortal hand or eye
> Could frame thy fearful symmetry?
>
> In what distant deeps or skies
> Burnt the fire of thine eyes?
> On what wings dare he aspire?
> What the hand dare sieze the fire?
>
> And what shoulder, & what art,
> Could twist the sinews of thy heart?

And when thy heart began to beat,
What dread hand? & what dread feet?

What the hammer? what the chain?
In what furnace was thy brain?
What the anvil? what dread grasp
Dare its deadly terrors clasp?

When the stars threw down their spears,
And watered heaven with their tears,
Did he smile his work to see?
Did he who made the Lamb make thee?

Tyger, Tyger, burning bright
In the forests of the night,
What immortal hand or eye
Dare frame thy fearful symmetry?

"The Tyger" is the most famous of Blake's poems. Its rhythm is like the beating of a hammer on an anvil as the tyger is forged "in the forests of the night." It is a poem composed of questions, which reach their climax in the question "Did he who made the Lamb make thee?" As for the answer, Blake leaves that to the reader. (Both "The Lamb" and "The Tyger" are reproduced in color on the end-papers of this book.)

It became Blake's practice to bind *Songs of Innocence* and *Songs of Experience* together as a way of "Showing the Two Contrary States of the Human Soul."

While the world of Innocence is one of protection and care, that of Experience seeks to confine and constrain the human spirit. As always, it is the lives of children that most move Blake. The poem "Infant Sorrow" uses the practice of swaddling newborns as a symbol of the bindings of Experience.

Songs of Experience, *title page, 1794.*
(Please see back endpapers for color repro-
duction of this image.)

Another bound infant appears on the frontispiece of *The Gates of Paradise*, on which William was also working at this time.

Swaddling was practised in the mistaken belief that it would "mend the shape" of the child. The newborn was tightly wound in a ten-foot-long strip of bandage until it could move neither arms nor legs. Dr. William Buchan, a contemporary of Blake who campaigned against the practice, wrote that "England would hardly know such a thing as a deformed child" if only parents would stop manacling their children.

There were a startling number of deserted children in Blake's London,

"The Chimney Sweeper," from Songs of
Experience, *1794.*

either abandoned by their parents, or given into the care of the local parish.
Although many were shipped off to factories in the north, parish children were
apprenticed to any number of appalling situations within the city itself. Blake
highlighted the desperate plight of the chimney sweeps in "The Chimney
Sweeper," another poem from *Songs of Experience*.

For twenty or thirty shillings, master sweepers took children as young as five
years old from parents desperate to feed their families. The smaller the child the
better, for the horrific job of the climbing boys was to negotiate the twists and
turns of the narrow chimneys, to sweep out the soot, and to put out the fires

that frequently flared. The smaller boy was often prodded on by another boy behind him with a pin. Sometimes boys became trapped, unable to move forward or back, and died by fire or suffocation.

Coated in black soot from head to toe, they often went unwashed for years. Few reached adulthood. The sight of these wretched children was common in the streets of London in Blake's day as they "called the streets" with their cry of "Sweep! Sweep!" They find their place in the poems of Experience.

A little black thing among the snow:
Crying, weep, weep, in notes of woe.

Songs of Experience was an indictment of the dark world that had descended on so many lives. Blake did something that had not been done before. He took these small lives and showed that their tragedies were as worthy of note as any other.

※

The years at Lambeth were the most fruitful of Blake's life. Book followed on book. He composed upon the plate as inspiration came. With pen and brush he took the narrow compass of the copper plate "and open'd its centre/ Into infinitude and ornamented it with wondrous art."

William and Catherine worked as a team, printing perhaps a dozen copies of each new book from the prepared plates. More could always be printed as the stock on hand dwindled. Generally, he would ink the plates in pairs and center them on the press bed. She would take the paper, dampened the day before and pressed between boards, and lay it down on the plates. Plates and paper would be covered with a backing sheet and two or three woolen pads. Then, slowly, they turned the large spoked wheel to move the rollers and bring the press bed between the cylinders, where the inked image was forced into the dampened fibers of the paper.

Speed was essential, for the ink dried quickly on the plates. William and

Inking, wiping, printing, and hanging line engravings, from an early engraving manual. The Blakes would have used a similar procedure when printing Illuminated Books.

Catherine hung the printed sheets on lines to dry, then painted each design by hand with watercolors. William ground his own colors from blocks of pigment, mixing the ground color with gum water, glycerine, honey, and ox gall to form a paste, which he then diluted with water to the proper consistency.

Once painted, he touched up the pages with pen and ink to add definition to the designs and to mend any flaws in the letters. Finally, Catherine collated and stitched together the pages between pale blue wrappers, using stab holes and string.

By 1793, Blake had created seven Illuminated Books. To publicize them, he issued a prospectus, addressed "To the Public." In announcing the work he had for sale, he explained that he had invented a method of printing which "combines the Painter and the Poet," and made the high claim that the works he had produced were of "equal consequence with the productions of any age or country."

The sales of most of Blake's Illuminated Books were meager. Of the joint *Songs of Innocence and of Experience*, little more than two dozen copies have survived, and it is likely that not many more were originally printed. Of the other books, sales were considerably fewer. But in Blake's vision, just as the small were large, so the few were many.

Over the next two years, he created five more books. His scope was larger than in *Songs*, but his concerns were the same: the fall from the freedom of imagination into the restraints of reason, from the opening of vision to its narrowing.

Meanwhile, to bring in much-needed money, William continued to take on engraving work. But the more he devoted his time and energy to his own creations, the less willing he became to bend his imagination to someone else's. When he engraved from his own designs, he let his imagination loose, as he did in the creation of his own books. The results were not always pleasing to his contemporaries.

Even his friends were disturbed by the extravagant turn his designs had taken. By the mid-1790s, his commissions were drying up and he and Catherine were in difficult circumstances.

Just at this pressing moment, William received the largest commission he had ever been offered. He was hired by Richard Edwards, a young book dealer and publisher, to illustrate a four-volume folio edition of Edward Young's *Night Thoughts*, one of the most popular poems of the time.

It was an ambitious and, in many ways, a perilous project. Folio was the largest size of book, and very expensive to produce. For a young publisher, employing a next-to-unknown engraver who had never designed on such a large scale, the venture was almost foolhardy. Edwards must have felt that the popularity of the poem would sell the book.

The sprightly lark's shrill matin wakes the morn,
Grief's sharpest thorn hard pressing on my breast;
I strive, with wakeful melody, to cheer
The sullen gloom, sweet philomel! like thee,
And call the stars to listen; every star
Is deaf to mine, enamour'd of thy lay:
Yet be not vain; there are, who thine excel,
And charm through distant ages: wrapp'd in shade,
Pris'ner of darkness! to the silent hours,
How often I repeat their rage divine,
To lull my griefs, and steal my heart from woe!
I roll their raptures, but not catch their fire:
Dark, though not blind, like thee Mæonides!
Or, Milton! thee; ah, could I reach your strain!
Or his, who made Mæonides our own:
Man too he sung—immortal man I sing:
* Oft bursts my song beyond the bounds of life;
What now, but immortality, can please?
O had he press'd his theme, pursued the track,
Which opens out of darkness into day!
O had he mounted on his wing of fire,
Soar'd, where I sink, and sung immortal man!
How had it bless'd mankind, and rescued me!

An engraving from Night Thoughts, *1797. Blake shows the poet drawn by inspiration to the world above, yet bound to the world below. The design illustrates the asterisked line.*

Blake was to make his initial designs in watercolor, from which Edwards would choose some two hundred to be engraved. Blake asked one hundred guineas for the watercolor work, but Edwards said he could not afford to pay him more than twenty. Blake accepted, no doubt believing that he stood to make on the engravings what he had lost on the watercolors.

Over the next two years, he worked almost exclusively on this project, painting an astounding 537 watercolors. From these, Edwards selected 43 to be engraved for the first volume. But by the time it was published in the fall of 1797, Edwards had totally lost interest in both the project and the publishing business. There was very little advertising, no review copies were sent out, and no reviews appeared. The plans for the final three volumes were quietly abandoned.

Edwards must have realized that the market for such an expensive book had dwindled. The next year he sold off his shop and accepted a government post.

Blake was crushed by the failure of the book. This vast project, on which he had spent so much time and energy, hoping it would bring critical and financial success, ended in a whimper.

Following the failure of *Night Thoughts*, there was talk again of Blake's extravagances. John Hoppner, a member of the Royal Academy, said his designs in the book were "like the conceits of a drunken fellow or a madman." What most shocked people was Blake's depiction of the spiritual world in physical terms. It was a complaint that would follow him throughout his life.

Even most of those friends who had been sympathetic and supplied William with engraving commissions dropped from view. In a letter to his friend George Cumberland in August 1799, he wrote

As to Myself, about whom you are so kindly Interested, I live by Miracle. I am Painting small Pictures from the Bible. For as to Engraving, in which art I cannot reproach myself with any neglect, yet I am laid by in a corner as if I did not Exist, & since my Young's Night Thoughts have been publish'd, even Johnson and Fuseli have discarded my Graver. But as I know that He who Works and has his health cannot starve, I laugh at Fortune & Go on & on.

Those few friends who stood by Blake struggled to help him. After a long stay in Italy, John Flaxman had returned to London. As a special present for his wife's birthday, he commissioned Blake to illustrate in watercolors the works of the poet Thomas Gray. He obtained a recent edition of the poems. Blake cut out the pages and centered them in windows cut into the large leftover sheets of the *Night Thoughts* stock. He then painted around each poem. Mrs. Flaxman was delighted with the gift.

George Cumberland, in an effort to help out, introduced William to Reverend John Trusler. Trusler, a prolific author of such books as *The Way to be Rich and Respectable*, was working on a book and needed an artist to design some "moral paintings" for it. He commissioned Blake to do two paintings, *Malevolence* and *Benevolence*. *Pride* and *Humility* were to follow, and then the four were to be engraved for the book.

Blake began the first painting, *Malevolence*. Reverend Trusler had given him some suggestions, and for two weeks Blake struggled to comply. When the painting would not come, he decided to follow his own inspiration and paint a scene that he felt would capture the spirit of malevolence perfectly. He sent it off to Reverend Trusler along with a letter explaining his actions and describing the scene:

A Father, taking leave of his Wife & Child, Is watch'd by two Fiends incarnate, with intention that when his back is turned they will murder the mother & her infant. If this is not Malevolence with a vengeance, I have never seen it on Earth; & if you approve of this, I have no doubt of giving you Benevolence with Equal Vigor, as also Pride & Humility.

Trusler definitely did not approve. He sent back the painting, and wrote that it did not meet his intentions:

Malevolence, 1799, *painted on approval for Reverend Trusler.*

Your Fancy, from what I have seen of it . . . seems to be in the other world, or the World of Spirits, which accords not with my Intentions, which, whilst living in This World, Wish to follow the Nature of it.

Blake responded to Reverend Trusler's letter with one of his own:

Revd Sir,
I really am sorry that you are fall'n out with the Spiritual World, Especially if I should have to answer for it. I feel very sorry that your Ideas & Mine on Moral Painting differ so much as to have made you angry with my method of Study. If I am wrong, I am wrong in good company. . . . You say that I want somebody to Elucidate my Ideas. But you ought to know that What is Grand is necessarily obscure to Weak men. That which can be made Explicit to the Idiot is not worth my care. The wisest of the Ancients consider'd what is not too Explicit as the fittest for Instruction, because it rouzes the faculties to act. . . .

I know that This World Is a World of Imagination & Vision. I see Every thing I paint In This World, but Every body does not see alike. To the eyes of a Miser a Guinea is more beautiful than the Sun, & a bag worn with the use of Money has more beautiful proportions than a Vine filled with Grapes. The tree which moves one to tears of joy is in the Eyes of others only a Green thing that stands in the way. Some see Nature all Ridicule & Deformity, & by these I shall not regulate my proportions; & Some Scarce see Nature at all. But to the Eyes of the Man of Imagination, Nature is Imagination itself. As a man is, So he Sees.

Blake and Reverend Trusler went their separate ways.
William and Catherine's prospects in London looked dim. They longed to make a new start. And suddenly the chance for that came their way.

CHAPTER EIGHT

FELPHAM AND WILLIAM HAYLEY

MY SON! MY SON!

OHN FLAXMAN WAS A LONGTIME FRIEND OF THE POPULAR poet William Hayley. Hayley's poem *The Triumphs of Temper*, published some twenty years earlier, had run to fourteen editions and brought him fame. Hayley called himself the Bard of Sussex and, from his country estate in Felpham, he loosed a steady stream of poems, plays, and biographies upon the world. He prided himself on the ease with which he wrote, and would commonly turn out four stanzas before breakfast.

The poet Southey said of him, "Everything about that man is good – except his poetry." Some years before, Hayley had befriended the poet William Cowper and supported him through the periods of madness that punctuated

A painting of Blake's friend John Flaxman modeling a bust of William Hayley, while Hayley's son Thomas looks on.

Cowper's life. Yet tempered with his kindness was a tendency to meddle with the work of his fellow artists for the purpose of "mending" it.

Hayley was a tall man, with a military manner. As a result of a childhood illness, he walked with a limp. When he went riding, he often carried a parasol and, in opening it, he sometimes startled his horse and was sent toppling to the ground.

His son Thomas had been steeped in art from an early age. At fourteen, he was apprenticed to John Flaxman to study the art of sculpture. But three years later, he was stricken with a degenerative disease of the spine and was forced to return home.

His father was distraught. As a tribute to the boy and his teacher, he composed a long poetical *Essay on Sculpture* in the form of a series of letters to John Flaxman. The book was to be illustrated by three engravings – two from drawings by his son of classical subjects, and the other from a medallion portrait of the boy by his teacher. On Flaxman's recommendation, Blake was hired to make the engravings.

As Thomas's health worsened, Hayley grew more and more anxious that the engraving of his son be completed, in hopes that the boy might "see his own engraved portrait arrive before his own departure."

At the beginning of April 1800, Blake sent off a proof. Hayley was unhappy with it, believing his son appeared "sullen." He sent it back for revisions – and then further revisions. Blake was still laboring to produce a portrait acceptable to Hayley, when, in early May, the boy died. Four days later, Blake sent off the revised proof along with a heartfelt letter of condolence:

Dear Sir,
I am very sorry for your immense loss which is a repetition of what all feel in this valley of misery & happiness mixed. I send the Shadow of the departed Angel: hope the likeness is improved. . . . I know that our deceased friends are more really with us than when they were apparent to our mortal part. Thirteen years ago I lost a brother & with his Spirit I converse daily & hourly in the Spirit & See him in my remembrance in the regions of my Imagination. I hear his advice & even now write from his Dictate. Forgive me for Expressing to you my Enthusiasm which I wish all to partake of Since it is to me a Source of Immortal Joy: even in this world by it I am the companion of Angels. May you continue to be so more & more & to be more & more persuaded that every Mortal loss is an Immortal Gain. The Ruins of Time builds Mansions in Eternity.

Blake's engraving of the medallion portrait of Hayley's son Thomas, 1800.

Some weeks later, Hayley, still not satisfied with the engraving, invited Blake to Turret House, his place in Felpham, to work with him on the portrait. His friend William Cowper had also recently died, and Hayley was busy planning a biography of the poet to memorialize him.

The two worked together in Hayley's new library, located in the turret from which the house took its name. Blake extended his stay. They got on so well that Hayley suggested that Blake rent a nearby vacant cottage, so they could continue to work closely together.

Blake's prospects in London were at a low ebb. Lately he had found himself plunged into "a deep pit of Melancholy." The chance for a change of life and the promise of a kindly patron were too tempting to pass up. Late in July, he rented a six-room thatched cottage from the landlord of the local inn and, in high spirits, prepared for the move. "It is to you I owe all my present happiness," he wrote to Flaxman. And to Hayley, "My fingers emit sparks of Fire with expectation of my future labours."

Sparks of a different sort would likely have flown had Blake seen a letter written by Flaxman to Hayley that August:

> I hope that Blake's residence in Felpham will be a Mutual Comfort to you & him, & I see no reason why he should not make as good a livelihood there as in London, if he engraves & teaches drawing, by which he may gain considerably as also by making neat drawings of different kinds, but if he places any dependence on painting large pictures, for which he is not qualified either by habit or study, he will be miserably deceived.

Early on the morning of September 18, 1800, William and Catherine boarded a coach and left Lambeth behind, looking forward to a new life in the country. They brought all their household belongings with them, as well as the dismantled wooden press, the heavy copper plates for his Illuminated Books, several portfolios of prints, and William's manuscripts and books and engraving tools. Sixteen heavy boxes in all.

Blake's sister came along to help with the move. Though Felpham was only sixty miles away, the trip lasted until nearly midnight, for they had to switch chaise and driver seven times, unloading and reloading their luggage each time. Still, they "travel'd thro' a most beautiful country on a most glorious day," as Blake wrote to his friend Thomas Butts. "All upon the road was cheerfulness & welcome; tho' our luggage was very heavy there was no grumbling at all."

William and Catherine were delighted with their new cottage, with their rustic neighbors, with the sights and smells of the countryside and the sea. On the morning after the move, as he was going out his gate, Blake saw a plowman and his son at work in the field. "Father, the Gate is open," called the boy. To

The cottage in Felpham, where the Blakes lived from 1800 to 1803.

Blake it seemed a sign that in this happy setting he would find the way open for his art.

"I call myself now Independent," he wrote to George Cumberland. "I can be Poet, Painter and Musician as the Inspiration comes."

All went well for a time. The couple set up house in the new cottage. There were three rooms and a kitchen on the ground floor, and three bedrooms on the upper floor, with a view across fields to the sea. For Catherine, it was like a step back to her life in Battersea. "The sweet air & the voices of winds, trees & birds, & the odours of the happy ground, makes it a dwelling for immortals," Blake wrote to a friend.

Each day he would leave the small cottage and make the short trek along the lane, past the local inn, to Hayley's villa. He went in through the gate in the high wall, passed through the surrounding gardens, and spent the day working

Geoffrey Chaucer, *one of the eighteen portraits Blake painted for Hayley's library, 1800–01.*

alongside Hayley in the library at the top of the turret, which commanded a view of the countryside and the sea.

One of the first tasks Hayley gave his "good Blake" was to design and paint eighteen oval portraits of famous literary figures to decorate the walls of the library. They included Homer, Shakespeare, Sidney, Spenser, Chaucer, and Cowper. Five of the portraits were from drawings by Hayley's departed son, Thomas, whose own self-portrait, copied by Blake, took pride of place above the mantelpiece.

The paintings were done in tempera, the heads surrounded by Blake's designs. Shakespeare was encircled by spirits; Chaucer, set within a laurel wreath and flanked by two Canterbury pilgrims, may have planted the seed for Blake's later engraving of the Canterbury Pilgrims.

Hayley was so pleased with the portraits that he urged Blake to try his hand at miniature portraits, and began drumming up business among his friends and neighbors. But his letter to a neighbor, to whom he was sending a miniature of his late wife by Blake, suggests that Hayley had little understanding of Blake's talent or temperament:

Mr dear Tom intended to execute for you such a Resemblance of Mrs. H_____. His own calamitous Illness & Death precluded Him from that pleasure – I have recently formed a new artist for this purpose by teaching a worthy creature (by profession an Engraver) who lives in a little Cottage very near me to paint in miniature.

And so this "recently formed" artist set about painting miniatures in and around Sussex. He soon found himself overwhelmed with orders.

Blake was also kept busy with engraving commissions for Hayley. The cottage, with its low-hanging thatched roof, was quite dark, so he spent most of his working days in Hayley's company. Through the following year, as Hayley worked on his *Life of Cowper*, Blake busied himself with the engravings for the book.

Lady Hesketh, Cowper's cousin, had a controlling interest in the project and was adamant that no hint of the poet's madness appear in the book. She found Blake's portrait of the poet from a drawing by Romney "dreadful! Shocking!" for precisely this reason.

Blake had a deep sympathy for the tormented Cowper and saw his insanity as a "refuge from unbelief" in a rationalistic age. Blake knew all too well how the spiritual fervor in his own work had laid him open to the same charge.

In the end, the engraving of the poet was allowed to stand, along with three others Blake completed for the book. Catherine had become such an accomplished printer that she printed all the plates for the work on their wooden press, which they had set up in the cottage.

This compelling self-portrait of Blake only came to light in 1974. It dates from the time he was painting miniatures for Hayley, c. 1803. The oval shape is traditional for miniatures.

Materially, the couple was prospering. William was doing his best to bind himself to the world of duty and reality, as his friends had advised him to do if he hoped to thrive. However, things were far from blissful for the Blakes.

Health concerns were becoming a very real problem. The low-lying cellar-less cottage was always damp, and Catherine began to suffer from severe rheumatism. As time passed, both she and William were frequently confined to bed with fever, unable to work.

In addition, Blake and Hayley's relationship had grown increasingly strained. Hayley seemed to regard William as little more than his hired assistant, his paid companion. He was friendly enough, but the relationship was clearly not on an equal footing, and Blake came to realize that "corporeal friends" could be "spiritual enemies."

While his own work languished for lack of time, William had to read to Hayley, listen to his poetry, draw designs from his sketches, and accompany him on his constant errands around the countryside – with Hayley riding ahead on his horse and Blake following along on his pony. When he was hired to give drawing lessons to Lady Bathurst's children, she asked him if he would paint a set of handscreens for her – a commission he found so demeaning that he declined it.

All in all, it is hard to see how so fiercely independent a spirit as Blake was able to endure the stifling atmosphere of Felpham for so long. What seems to have finally brought matters to a head was yet another of Hayley's schemes for finding work by which his friend might turn a profit. Hayley proposed to write a series of ballads relating to animals. He tossed off these trite pieces for Blake's amusement as Blake labored on the engravings for the *Life of Cowper*.

His plan was to give these poems to Blake, who would illustrate each ballad with three engravings of his own design. Blake would publish the poems singly in fifteen monthly installments. The profits would be his, and when the series was complete, the poems would be collected and published as a book.

As publisher, Blake was to shoulder the costs of the paper and printing. Joseph Seagrave, a businessman and friend of Hayley, was to print the text.

The Dog, *one of Blake's engravings for Hayley's* Ballads, *1805. The design was ridiculed by the poet Southey: "The delectable frontispiece . . . represents Edward starting back,* Fido volant, *and the* crocodile rampant, *with a mouth open like a bootjack to receive him."*

William and Catherine would later add the engravings, printed on their own press.

Only four poems in the proposed series were ever issued – "The Elephant," "The Eagle," "The Lion," and "The Dog." Asking his well-placed friends for assistance, Hayley tried to help with the sales but soon grew discouraged at the lukewarm response and lost interest. Blake, who had invested considerable time and money in the venture, was left to absorb the loss. Hayley blamed the failure on Blake being "not very fit to manage pecuniary concerns to his own advantage." But Blake no doubt felt he had been promised a good deal more help than he received.

He had come to Felpham with high hopes of beginning a new life. He had looked forward to having the freedom to create his own work in an idyllic country setting. He had seen those hopes dashed and found himself in much the same situation in Felpham that he had fled in London.

William unburdened himself in a letter to his friend Thomas Butts in January 1802:

> When I came down here, I was more sanguine than I am at present; but it was because I was ignorant of many things which have since occurred, & chiefly the unhealthiness of the place. . . .
>
> But you have so generously & openly desired that I will divide my griefs with you, that I cannot hide what it is now become my duty to explain. . . . I find on all hands great objections to my doing any thing but the mere drudgery of business, & intimations that if I do not confine myself to this, I shall not live; this has always pursued me. . . . This from Johnson & Fuseli brought me down here, and this from Mr. H. will bring me back again; for that I cannot live without doing my duty to lay up treasures in heaven is Certain & Determined. . . . if we fear to do the dictates of our Angels, & Tremble at the Tasks set before us; if we refuse to

do Spiritual Acts because of Natural Fears or Natural Desires! Who can describe the dismal torments of such a state. . . . But I am now no longer in That State, & now go on again with my Task, Fearless, and tho' my path is difficult, I have no fear of stumbling while I keep it.

In 1799, when it seemed to Blake that he had been "laid by in a corner as if [he] did not exist," it had been Butts who had given him the commission for a series of small biblical paintings at a guinea apiece. Since moving to Felpham, he had been so busy with work for Hayley that he been unable to find time to finish those paintings.

Now he returned to that task and, in November 1802, sent two more paintings off to Butts. In the quiet of the country, Blake had been able to recollect his scattered thoughts on art, and had resumed his "primitive and original ways of Execution in both painting and Engraving."

But the task that preoccupied him and often roused him in the night to work on was a long poem he had begun to compose while living in Lambeth. He called it *Vala*, though later he retitled it *The Four Zoas*. It was by far the longest poem he had ever written, close to four thousand lines in the revised version. "I have written this poem from immediate Dictation, twelve and sometimes twenty or thirty lines at a time," he wrote to Butts. "I mention this to show what I think the grand reason for my being brought down here."

Vala was the vast cluttered workshop where Blake molded the elements of the myth that would form the structure for his later work. The poem's opening lines are

Four Mighty Ones are in every Man: a perfect Unity
Cannot Exist but from the Universal Brotherhood of Eden,
The Universal Man, to Whom be Glory Evermore.

Blake called this universal man Albion. And the four mighty ones who are in him are the Four Zoas, his four eternal powers. He named them Urizen ("your reason"), Los (the spirit of imagination and poetry), Luvah ("lover," who dwells in the human heart), and Tharmas (the five senses, the physical body).

The poem explores the fall of these powers into fragmentation and their final restoration to unity. It picks up where the Illuminated Books had left off, in a dark world dominated by Urizen, "the great Work master," who proclaims himself God. Some of the poem's most powerful lines are an indictment of the ills of industrialism – always tied in Blake's mind to war – and a lament for the loss of craft:

> Then left the sons of Urizen the plow & harrow, the loom,
> The hammer & the chisel & the rule & compasses.
> They forg'd the sword, the chariot of war, the battle ax,
> The trumpet fitted to the battle & the flute of summer,
> And all the arts of life they chang'd into the arts of death.
> The hour glass contemn'd because its simple workmanship
> Was as the workmanship of the plowman, & the water wheel
> That raises water into Cisterns, broken & burn'd in fire
> Because its workmanship was like the workmanship of the shepherd,
> And in their stead intricate wheels invented, Wheel without wheel,
> To perplex youth in their outgoings & to bind to labours
> Of day & night the myriads of Eternity, that they might file
> And polish brass & iron hour after hour, laborious workmanship,
> Kept ignorant of the use that they might spend the days of wisdom
> In sorrowful drudgery to obtain a scanty pittance of bread.

William made the mistake of showing part of the poem to Hayley, who looked on it "with sufficient contempt to enhance my opinion of it." Blake was determined "to be no longer pestered with his Genteel Ignorance and Polite Disapprobation. I know myself both Poet and Painter, and it is not his affected Contempt that can move me to any thing but a more assiduous pursuit of both Arts."

And so, in the spring of 1803, Blake decided to return to London. He announced it to Butts in a letter of April 25:

Now I may say to you, what perhaps I should not dare to say to any one else: That I can alone carry on my visionary studies in London unannoy'd, and that I may converse with my friends in Eternity, see Visions, Dream Dreams, & prophesy & speak Parables unobserv'd and at liberty from the Doubts of other Mortals.

However, just prior to the Blakes' departure, an incident occurred which could well have had disastrous consequences.

After a year of uneasy peace, England and France were once again at war, and even the sleepy village of Felpham was not beyond its reach. That summer a troop of the First Regiment of the Royal Dragoons was lodging at the Fox Inn. The regiment had been assembled in the area to prepare for a possible invasion of French forces along the Sussex coast.

On Friday, August 12, one of the soldiers ventured into Blake's garden to help the gardener who was working there. Blake was indoors writing. He heard voices and, on coming out to investigate, discovered the soldier in the garden. Not knowing the circumstances, he asked him to leave. The soldier refused, and heated words were exchanged.

Blake then took the soldier by the elbows and pushed him out through the gate. And when the soldier threatened him, he pushed him along the road another fifty yards as far as the Fox Inn, whose owner, Mr. Grinder, was Blake's landlord. Further insults were exchanged and a companion of the soldier, lodged at the inn, also became involved. Finally, the innkeeper managed to separate the men, sending Blake home and urging the soldiers inside.

The outraged and humiliated soldier, Private John Schofield, charged Blake with assault and uttering seditious words. Given the uneasy temper of the times, with the Napoleonic Wars raging in Europe and England herself fearing a French invasion, sedition was a serious charge, punishable by imprisonment and fine.

Hayley immediately came to his friend's aid. He put forward money for Blake's bail and hired a lawyer, his friend Samuel Rose, to act in his defense. In October, Blake appeared at the Quarter Sessions at Petworth, where he heard the charges against him and pleaded Not Guilty. The trial was set for January 1804.

In the meantime, the Blakes had returned to London and lodged temporarily at the Blake family home on Broad Street with William's brother and sister. Catherine, already unwell, had been left "much terrified" under the weight of the charge against her husband.

Hayley had agreed to stand as one of the key witnesses at the trial, prepared to offer evidence of Blake's peaceful character. However, just a few days beforehand, he was out riding and his horse fell, throwing him headfirst to the ground. If not for the strong new hat he was wearing, he would have been seriously injured.

Over his doctor's objections, Hayley attended the trial and spoke on Blake's behalf, as did a number of his Felpham neighbors who had seen the incident. Midway through the trial, as Schofield altered the truth in support of his case, Blake called out in a loud voice, "False!", with such conviction that the courtroom was electrified. Years later, a man who had been present at the trial as a boy said that all he remembered of it was Blake's "flashing eye."

In the end, despite the onset of a sudden illness that prevented Blake's lawyer from continuing with his case, the jury acquitted Blake of all charges. The courtroom erupted in noisy rejoicing as the verdict was handed down.

CHAPTER NINE

SOUTH MOLTON STREET

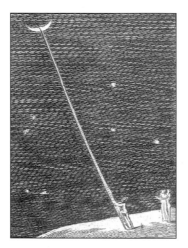

I WANT! I WANT!

 ITH THE "INFERNAL BUSINESS OF THE SOLDIER . . . GOT OVER," William and Catherine settled the sticks and feathers of their new nest in London. In the fall, while the trial still hung over their heads, they had moved into a second-floor flat at 17 South Molton Street. Now they unpacked and assembled their wooden press in the cramped new quarters. It was a far cry from their cottage in the country, with neither garden nor tree. From the front, they looked out on a row of houses and shops; from the back, they had a distant view of Hyde Park.

Catherine's health and strength began to return. At first, in gratitude for Hayley's efforts in his defense, William was busy running errands for him in the city, tracking down the paintings and drawings of George Romney, the subject

17 South Molton Street,
home of the Blakes from
1803 to 1821. While living
here, Blake wrote the poems
Milton *and* Jerusalem.

of a new biography by Hayley; and acting as Hayley's London agent in various business affairs. He found London had changed in the three years he'd been away. The streets were wider, neater, busier. A new spirit of commerce gripped the city. It had become "a City of Elegance in some degree. . . . There are now I believe as many Booksellers as there are Butchers and as many Printshops as of any other trade," he wrote to Hayley.

Blake could well remember when a print shop was a "rare bird" in London, back in the days when he and Parker had struggled to keep their small business afloat. But now the new buying public, eager for the latest fashions, converged on the print shops and bought art in the same spirit as they bought the newest styles in clothes or other goods.

The print merchants stocked their shops with large quantities of popular prints. The fashionable tonal style of engraving could be produced quickly in factory-style workshops to meet the public demand for prints that captured the events of the day. Engraving had been swept up in the new age of industry.

The print merchants, whose motive was profit, subtly shaped the taste of the buying public to those styles that were easiest and cheapest to produce. The fashionable "dotting" and "stippling" styles could be completed in a fraction of the time it took to do a line engraving, and most of the labor could be assigned to unskilled workers with little knowledge of drawing.

As commerce thrived, craft declined, and skilled engravers such as Blake were left to fend for themselves. "No one brings work to me," Blake lamented, so "I suppose that I must go a Courting, which I shall do awkwardly." He renewed his contacts with Johnson and Flaxman, which resulted in commissions for a few commercial plates, but, by and large, he found that those who used to bring him work had in his absence gone elsewhere, or had turned to the newer, cheaper methods. Even the commissions he expected from Hayley in return for running his errands dwindled to next to nothing. He was in dire straights. But, fortunately, he had a savior.

Thomas Butts, Blake's friend and patron. Miniature on ivory by Blake, 1801.

In Thomas Butts, Blake found not only a faithful friend, but a generous patron who believed in his visionary art and allowed him the liberty to exercise it. For over twenty years, Butts purchased at a moderate price everything Blake painted for him, until the walls of his house were covered with Blake's paintings. For many years, he was the one man who, in Samuel Palmer's words, "stood between the greatest designer in England and the Workhouse."

Their arrangement was a simple one. Butts would advance Blake a little money as he needed it, and Blake would repay him with paintings. From 1803 to 1810, Butts paid Blake over four hundred pounds for paintings and for engraving lessons for his son Tommy.

Butts was more than simply a patron; he was a friend. In the dark days in Felpham, Blake was able to pour out his most secret thoughts in his letters to Butts. Now that the Blakes were back in London, the two families socialized again. William and Catherine were regular visitors to the Buttses' large house on Great Marlborough Street.

Butts held a government post. He was Chief Clerk in the office of the Commissary General of Musters. He was responsible for writing letters dealing with the enlistment of soldiers, with ensuring that their equipment was in order, with issuing soldiers their pay, and with ensuring that those being paid were, in fact, alive and in uniform. It was a difficult and exacting job, and Butts was paid well for it. As with most government positions, the job came with a number of generous privileges. Butts invested his money wisely – in real estate, mining, and railroads – and by his death in 1845, was a wealthy man.

It is difficult to say why a seemingly conventional figure such as Thomas Butts was drawn to someone as radical as Blake. At levels deeper than how they earned their money, their spirits were in harmony. They got on.

Now, as Butts advanced him small sums of money to make ends meet, William devoted his energies to completing the first series of fifty paintings of illustrations to the Bible. Then, as he was about to begin a second series, he experienced a sudden vision that transformed both his life and his work.

⁂

It occurred in the fall of 1804, following his visit to the Truchsessian Gallery, where he saw works by those Renaissance masters he had so admired in his youth. It seemed that time suddenly fell away and

I was again enlightened with the light I enjoyed in my youth, which has for exactly twenty years been closed from me as by a door and by window shutters. . . . I am really drunk with intellectual vision whenever I take a pencil or graver into my hand, even as I used to be in my youth.

106

The Lord answers Job out of
the Whirlwind, *watercolor
c. 1803–05. Blake would return
to the story of Job repeatedly
throughout his life.*

Restored "to the light of Art," Blake painted now with a renewed fervor and
vision. He worked in bright watercolors rather than the dark tempera treat-
ments he had used for the first series of biblical paintings. As if symbolic of his
own spiritual rebirth, he chose such subjects as *The Resurrection, The Trans-
figuration,* and *The Raising of Lazarus.*

One of his most beautiful pictures, *The Lord answers Job out of the Whirlwind,* dates from this period and may have been the inspiration for the series
of illustrations to the Book of Job that Blake would later paint for Butts.

Blake also took out the plate of *Glad Day,* which he had engraved more than
twenty years before. He reworked the plate, burnishing it extensively and
engraving lines of radiance around the figure, so that it seemed to glow from

within. Beneath the figure he engraved the words, "Albion rose from where he laboured at the Mill with Slaves. . . ."

He felt that he, too, had been like "a slave bound in a mill." The new industrial order that had enslaved so many of the poor and powerless had caught him and his craft up in its grasp. "They cause that everything in Art shall become a Machine," he lamented. He rejected it.

"I throw Myself & all that I have on our Saviour's Divine Providence," he wrote to Hayley. Come what may, he gave himself over to "the Use of that Talent which it is Death to Bury," the exercise of his gifts as painter and poet.

Fired with renewed enthusiasm, Blake began work on his first Illuminated Books in nine years. He designed and printed the title pages of the two long poems that would occupy much of his creative energies for the next sixteen years, *Milton* and *Jerusalem*.

He had begun work on the text of *Milton* while still at Felpham. The poem is a celebration of imagination and vision over reason and rule. Blake's intention was "to cast aside from Poetry all that is not Inspiration." For he believed that to speak according to inspiration was to speak truth.

In a poem whose purpose was to liberate imagination, Blake ignored the conventions that dictated how a story should be told – with events arranged in linear order, places fixed at separate points in space, and characters confined to distinct and separate selves. In *Milton*, these rules do not apply. Time and space are subject to imagination; characters shift identity, split apart, flow together; everything is happening everywhere at once.

In the preface to the poem, Blake addresses the young artists of the New Age. He urges them to "rouze up," to shake off the old order, and to be "just and true" to their own imaginations. It is a stirring call to action, and it concludes with one of Blake's most moving lyrics, known to many now as the song "Jerusalem."

And did those feet in ancient time
Walk upon England's mountains green?

And was the holy Lamb of God
On England's pleasant pastures seen?

And did the Countenance Divine
Shine forth upon our clouded hills?
And was Jerusalem builded here
Among these dark Satanic Mills?

Bring me my Bow of burning gold:
Bring me my Arrows of desire:
Bring me my Spear: O clouds unfold!
Bring me my Chariot of fire.

I shall not cease from Mental Fight,
Nor shall my Sword sleep in my hand
Till we have built Jerusalem
In England's green and pleasant land.

Blake admired John Milton above all other poets. Yet he believed Milton had erred in placing reason above imagination. He felt that this error had marred Milton's poetic vision and his personal life. In *Milton*, Blake allows the poet, "unhappy tho' in heaven," the chance to return to Earth to destroy his selfhood, reason, and to redeem his imagination. The poem is divided into two books, and contains approximately fifty copper plates.

At the heart of the poem, there stands a moment of vision. It occurred early one morning as Blake was walking in the garden of his cottage in Felpham. Milton seemed to descend from the heavens in the form of a falling star and, striking Blake's left foot, "entered there."

From this moment of vision, the poem unfolds like a flower. Some of the finest poetry in *Milton* is a celebration of such moments.

The spirit Ololon descends to Blake's cottage at Felpham. Milton, *plate 36, 1804–11.*
Blake is seen walking in the garden from which he ejected the soldier, Schofield.

Every Time less that a pulsation of the artery
Is equal in its period & value to Six Thousand Years,
For in this Period the Poet's Work is Done, and all the Great
Events of Time start forth & are conceiv'd in such a Period,
Within a Moment, a Pulsation of the Artery.

Blake always had the small at heart. Children, the poor, the tiny creatures of nature: it is these that had his love. Against the massive power of the "dark Satanic Mills" that confine the human spirit, he sets the stubborn, striving spirit of small things acting in harmony and joy.

In *Milton*, the symbol of this creative spirit is the lark, which springs with a loud trill from the waving cornfield and "leads the Choir of Day."

His little throat labours with inspiration; every feather
On throat & breast & wings vibrates with the effluence Divine.
All Nature listens silent to him, & the awful Sun
Stands still upon the Mountain looking on this little Bird
With eyes of soft humility & wonder, love & awe.
Then loud from their green covert all the Birds begin their Song:
The Thrush, the Linnet & the Goldfinch, Robin & the Wren
Awake the Sun from his sweet reverie upon the Mountain.
The Nightingale again assays his song, & thro' the day
And thro' the night warbles luxuriant, every Bird of Song
Attending his loud harmony with admiration & love.

Blake worked on *Milton* for seven years. Each plate was written and designed by hand, then printed and hand-colored. It is a work of art. Yet only four copies of the poem have survived, and it is likely that Blake sold no more than this. He was himself "a little bird" in the world's eyes. And yet, like the lark trilling its song, he, too, springs from the earth to lead "the Choir of Day."

It is a choir composed not of one voice but of many, each singing its own distinctive song, yet all contributing to one glorious harmony. This joyful unity in diversity is Blake's vision of the New Age.

But before its dawning, there were dark hours ahead.

CHAPTER TEN

THE GRAVE

HELP! HELP!

Y THE FALL OF 1805, BLAKE HAD HAD ENOUGH OF WILLIAM Hayley. He had grown tired of running errands for him in London. He had seen commissions he had hoped to receive from Hayley awarded to others. And a plan to publish in book form the *Ballads Relating to Animals* had left Blake seriously in debt. But no sooner had he freed himself from the smothering embrace of William Hayley than he walked straight into the clutches of Robert Cromek.

Cromek, a fellow engraver, had been a pupil of the famous Francesco Bartolozzi. Over the previous ten years, he had worked on a series of book illustrations from designs by Stothard and was greatly admired by Flaxman. But his health had always been fragile, and the exacting labor of engraving wore upon him. So, in 1804, he turned his hand to the business of book publishing instead. He had very little capital, but a keen business sense and a winning way. And he could be shrewd and unscrupulous if it served his interests.

In September 1805, possibly at the suggestion of Flaxman, Cromek approached Blake with his idea for his first venture into publishing – an illustrated edition of Robert Blair's poem *The Grave*. Blair, a Scottish minister, had published his poem in 1743, after the appearance of the first installment of Young's *Night Thoughts*. Both poems became immensely popular. They belong to the "graveyard school" of poetry, which dwelt on themes of mortality, and scenes such as abandoned churchyards and tombs.

William was delighted with the opportunity to express his own ideas on death and resurrection by illustrating Blair's poem. He accepted the commission and immediately set to work on the designs. In October, Flaxman wrote to Hayley:

> Mr. Cromek has employed Blake to make a set of 40 drawings from Blair's poem of *The Grave*, 20 of which he proposes to have engraved by the Designer and to publish them, with the hope of rendering Service to the Artist. Several members of the Royal Academy have been highly pleased with the specimens and mean to encourage the work.

Cromek paid Blake a pound apiece for the twenty designs he selected. It was not much, but Blake hoped to see a large profit when he engraved the designs. For to engrave even a single plate, he could charge as much as three times what he had been paid for all the designs.

With Blake's watercolor designs in hand, Cromek sought the support of several members of the Royal Academy and persuaded Fuseli to write a "puff" praising Blake's designs, which he printed in a prospectus advertising the project. While Blake worked busily on the first engraving, Cromek distributed the prospectus far and wide and signed on subscriptions. The response was enthusiastic, and all signs pointed to a great success.

Death's Door,
*1805, the white-
line engraving
Blake presented
to Cromek.*

Late in November, Blake delivered the finished first engraving, *Death's Door*, for Cromek's approval. Cromek did *not* approve. It was a white-line engraving – the lines stood white against a ground of black – and it had been done in the bold austere style Blake had rediscovered the year before. Whether Cromek voiced his disapproval directly to Blake is uncertain. What is certain is that, swiftly and without further ceremony, he went behind Blake's back, quietly signed on another engraver, and issued a revised prospectus.

The engraver was a friend and fellow pupil of Bartolozzi, Louis Schiavonetti, who employed the soft, stipple style that had become so fashionable. It was purely a business decision, but executed in a cold underhanded manner.

It was not long before Blake discovered he had been stripped of the commission for the engravings and robbed of the considerable profit he stood to make from the job. He was understandably furious. In his notebook, he scrawled these verses:

A petty sneaking Knave I knew
O Mr. C —— how do you do?

Cr —— loves artists as he loves his Meat
He loves the Art, but tis the Art to Cheat.

Cromek's smoothness somehow enabled him to calm Blake and even convince him that all had worked out for the best. It was, in the end, in both men's interests to maintain a civil relationship. Cromek was publishing Blake's designs, and Blake was seeing his work brought before a large discriminating public, thanks to Cromek's project. While the engravings were not to be his own, the designs were. And so it appears that an uneasy truce existed for a time between the two men.

That truce was shattered by a second incident. The consequences were to shape Blake's life over the next decade, and Robert Cromek stood squarely at the center of the affair.

Death's Door,
*Schiavonetti's
engraving from
Blake's design, 1808.
The aged man is
blown as if by a
tempest through
the door. Above, the
same figure is shown
reborn in youth
and glory.*

During 1806, while Schiavonetti was engraving the plates for *The Grave*, Cromek continued to call upon the Blakes. He and Blake must, on some level, have gotten on. Blake spoke his deepest thoughts to Cromek, and Cromek seemed sympathetic to his ideas. To experience such intellectual sympathy was rare for Blake, and he no doubt relished it and allowed it to calm his indignation at having been stripped of the engraving commission.

On one such visit, Cromek noticed a pencil sketch on the wall of Blake's workroom. The subject of the sketch was the procession of Chaucer's Canterbury Pilgrims. Chaucer was not as widely read then as now. However, Blake's interest in the poet dated back to his boyhood and, while employed by Hayley, he had painted a portrait of Chaucer, flanked by two Canterbury pilgrims on horseback, for Hayley's library.

Cromek was delighted with the originality of the sketch. He asked Blake if he would consider preparing a finished drawing of the piece, from which an engraving could be made. Having been so recently deceived, Blake was not about to negotiate with Cromek. Still, Cromek told him that if and when Blake finished the drawing, he would like to see it.

Shortly afterward, and with no mention of Blake's sketch on the same subject, Cromek approached Thomas Stothard and suggested he do a painting of Chaucer's Canterbury Pilgrims in procession. He may have made some suggestions for the design of the piece, drawn directly from Blake's treatment. With no notion of what was afoot, Stothard accepted the commission at a price of sixty pounds and set to work.

Relations between Blake and Stothard had been cool for some time. In the early years they had been close friends, and many of Blake's first commercial engravings had been from designs by Stothard. But they had quarreled, and after 1785, Blake never engraved from a Stothard design again. As recently as January 1803, Blake wrote to his brother James: "Hayley is as jealous as Stothard was and will no further be my friend than he is compelled by circumstances."

It seems unlikely, then, that Blake would have dropped by Stothard's studio and seen the painting in progress. It seems even less likely that, having seen it,

Pilgrimage to Canterbury, *oil painting by Stothard, 1806–07.*

Chaucer's Canterbury Pilgrims, *engraved by Blake from his painting of the same, 1810. It is very curious that Stothard's treatment of this unusual subject should be the same size and shape as Blake's, both designed to go over a mantelpiece.*

he would have praised it and "expressed much pleasure in seeing it," as Stothard later maintained. It is far more likely that both men went quietly about their work with no knowledge of what the other was doing.

It is quite possible, in fact, that Blake knew nothing of the entire affair until Stothard's painting was finished in the spring of 1807, when Cromek exhibited it to an enthusiastic public at a shilling apiece. Or he may have seen the painting in late January of that year and realized immediately that Cromek had cheated him yet again. This would explain the poignant entry in his notebook:

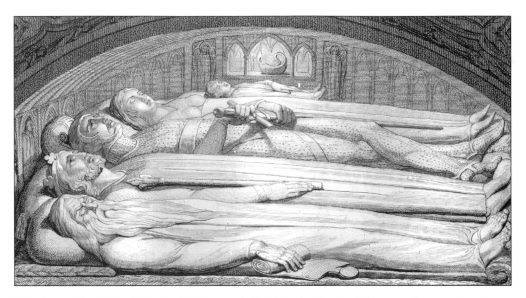

The Counsellor, King, Warrior, Mother and Child in the Tomb, *Schiavonetti's engraving from Blake's design for* The Grave, *1808. The figures resemble the marble effigies in Westminster Abbey that Blake sketched in his apprentice years.*

"Tuesday Janry. 20, 1807 between Two and Seven in the Evening – Despair."

It was not his despair, however, that Cromek and Stothard now witnessed, but his fury. Convinced that Stothard had been in on the business, Blake broke with him completely. He also severed relations with Flaxman, as Blake felt that Flaxman had unfairly taken Stothard's side in the affair. The two men saw nothing of each other for a long time afterwards.

In the summer of 1808, *The Grave* appeared, to largely unfavorable reviews. While Schiavonetti's skill as an engraver was praised, Blake's designs were thought indecent and absurd. His representation of the soul in bodily form again sparked shock and anger. "Absurd effusions," wrote *The Antijacobin Review*, "the offspring of a morbid fancy."

Still, on the basis of the seven hundred advance subscriptions alone, the book turned a handsome profit. Blake was to see nothing of it. Doubly insulting was the fact that, at the end of the book, a prospectus for an engraving by Schiavonetti of Stothard's Canterbury Pilgrims was inserted.

It was as if a curse lay over that entire project. In the midst of his work on the engraving, Schiavonetti was stricken with consumption and died in June 1810, at forty-five years of age. Less than two years later Cromek followed, struck down by the same disease. He was forty-two.

It was left to Cromek's widow, cast into desperate straits by her husband's death, and with two small children to care for, to raise the money to have the plate completed by selling off the rights to *The Grave*. The engraving, which was finally finished and offered for sale in 1817, was a huge success, and Cromek's widow was made a wealthy woman.

CHAPTER ELEVEN

THE EXHIBITION OF 1809:
"A MACHINE IS NOT A MAN"

AGED IGNORANCE

HE CROMEK AFFAIR WOUNDED WILLIAM DEEPLY. NOT ONLY had he lost over five hundred pounds for the engraving commission for *The Grave*, but his Chaucer design had been stolen from under his nose and turned to another's profit. His designs for *The Grave* had been ridiculed, and he had been personally attacked by the reviewers and accused of madness. Worst of all, he felt betrayed by those he thought were his friends.

He decided to take action. He would attempt to appeal to the public himself and prove his accusers wrong. Throughout the fall and winter of 1808, he prepared to mount a personal exhibition of his paintings. He wrote a detailed catalogue to accompany it, in which he laid out his views on art and answered the accusations against him.

So deeply involved was he in the project that when George Cumberland wrote to him in December saying that a friend wished to buy a complete set of Blake's Illuminated Books, Blake thanked him heartily but explained that he could not take up his "former pursuits of printing. . . . I have already involved myself in engagements that preclude all possibility of promising anything."

For all his deceitfulness, Cromek was a master at advertising and promoting his projects. He had shown Stothard's painting of the Canterbury Pilgrims in his house in Newman Street. More than three thousand people had paid to see it and received a copy of the prospectus for the forthcoming engraving.

Now as Blake mounted his own exhibition, where he would display his own painting of the Canterbury Pilgrims, he attempted some of Cromek's methods. His exhibition would also take place in a house, saving him the cost of renting expensive exhibition rooms. But there was no space for such an undertaking in his cramped flat in South Molton Street. He approached his brother James, who agreed to give over several rooms of the family home at 28 Broad Street to the exhibition.

The neighborhood had declined. The fashionable tenants of Golden Square had long since left, and their town houses been turned into flats for single men. James Blake may have hoped that visitors to the exhibition might bring along a little trade for his ailing haberdashery business.

Blake had an advertisement printed for the show, the motto of which – "Fit audience tho' few" – proved prophetic. The exhibition was to run from May to September, but extended well into the following year. There were few visitors. Among those who did find their way to Broad Street was the journalist and diarist Henry Crabb Robinson, who visited it in April 1810. He wrote:

> The paintings filled several rooms of an ordinary dwelling house. And for the Sight a half crown was demanded of the Visitor for which he also had a Catalogue. . . . I took four & giving 10s. bargained that I should be at liberty to go again. "Free! as long as you live," said the

The Penance of Jane Shore, c. 1779, an early watercolor drawing from Blake's days at the Royal Academy.

brother – astonished at such liberality, which he had never experienced before nor I dare say did afterwards.

The *Descriptive Catalogue* of the exhibit was a small volume of seventy-two pages, bound in gray paper wrappers. In it Blake not only commented on the paintings but set forth in strong language his views on art and artists. No more than fifty to a hundred copies were printed, but for many years the catalogue was the most widely quoted literary work by Blake. It is a document which, as his friend George Cumberland said, was "part vanity, part madness – part very good sense."

Among the paintings described in it was the largest piece that Blake ever painted, a huge canvas, now lost, entitled *The Ancient Britons*. It was larger than all the other paintings combined, measuring 10' × 14', and took up an entire wall.

There were fifteen other works on display. One of them, *The Penance of Jane Shore*, dated back to his days as a student at the Royal Academy, some thirty years before.

Still, the centerpiece of the exhibit was his painting of the Canterbury Pilgrims. And it was to this painting that he devoted the lion's share of his comments in the *Descriptive Catalogue*. Blake had been stung by the personal attack made on him by the reviewers of *The Grave*. A large part of his motive for launching the exhibition was to prove the critics wrong and bypass their power by appealing directly to the public. His *Canterbury Pilgrims* was painted, he wrote, "in self-defence against the insolent and envious imputation of unfitness for scientific art . . . most artfully and industriously . . . propagated among the public by ignorant hirelings."

He was sure that the painting "now exhibited will give the lie to such aspersions."

Those who visited the exhibit would have seen a painting that, while similar in many particulars, was quite different in spirit and execution to Stothard's. Blake's portrait was in tempera rather than oil, for this was the medium of the masters he admired. It is a deliberately old-fashioned picture, like something that might have been painted in Chaucer's own time. Blake researched the clothing that would have been worn by Chaucer's pilgrims, perhaps returning to Westminster Abbey to ensure that "the costume [was] correct according to authentic Monuments."

From the beginning Blake planned to make an engraving of the painting. One of his reasons for launching the exhibition, as had been the case in Cromek's exhibition of Stothard's Canterbury Pilgrims, was to drum up business for the engraving that was to follow.

Blake advertised the engraving in a prospectus released at the time the exhibition opened, promising it would be ready in one year's time. It was an enormous undertaking, for the finished engraving was to measure 1' × 3'. He gave copies of the prospectus to friends, print dealers, and those who attended the exhibition. Subscriptions for the engraving were received on-site.

Blake's comments on Chaucer's pilgrims are penetrating. "Of Chaucer's characters as described in his Canterbury Tales, some of the names and titles are altered by time, but the characters themselves remain unaltered. . . . Chaucer's characters live age after age. Every Age is a Canterbury Pilgrimage."

If Blake believed every age to be a Canterbury pilgrimage, then so, too, was his own. As he painted and later engraved this procession of pilgrims, was he tempted to include portraits of himself and his contemporaries among the nine and twenty that journey toward Canterbury?

He describes each character in turn. Among his pilgrims, Chaucer included a plowman. In Blake's work, plowing is a symbol for the coming of the New Age. He viewed his own craft as a kind of plowing because the graver cut through the copper like a plow, leaving furrows in its wake. The plowman in Blake's portrait looks remarkably like him, down to the broad-brimmed hat he commonly wore.

Also in the procession is a pardoner. Blake described him as "the Age's Knave," a term he had recently used to describe Robert Cromek. ("A petty sneaking Knave I knew . . .") The pardoner "is sent in every age for a rod and scourge; and for a blight, for a trial of man." The plowman plows and sows; the pardoner brings blight. One wonders whether Blake poured something of Robert Cromek into the figure of the pardoner.

While the painting was on display, Blake worked busily on the engraving. Since being stripped of the commission to engrave his designs for *The Grave*, he had not taken on any new commissions, and apart from his *Canterbury Pilgrims*, he was to abandon the craft entirely for over eight years. This engraving, then,

Chaucer's Canterbury Pilgrims *(detail). The plowman is the second figure from the left, in the broad-brimmed hat. The pardoner is the third from the right, looking over his left shoulder toward the plowman.*

marks a pivotal point in his life and represents a summation of all that he honored in his chosen craft. It is an homage to the school of line engraving in which he had been trained by Basire, similar in style to "the old original engravers, who were great masters in Painting and Designing."

He wanted to demonstrate to the public that he, as both artist and engraver, was best qualified to engrave from his own design. It was precisely this that he had been denied in the case of *The Grave*. And in the new commercial climate, it had become increasingly the rule that the artist provided the designs, while the actual engraving work was carried out by unskilled factory hands.

His engraving aims to reunite the two. It would be

minutely laboured, not by the Hands of Journeymen, but by the Original Artist himself, even to the Stuffs and Embroidery of the Garments, the hair upon the Horses, the Leaves upon the Trees, and the Stones and Gravel upon the road.

While he worked on these minute details of his engraving, Blake drafted in his notebook an address to the public on the state of art, and in particular of engraving, in England. This *Public Address* was his response to yet another project by Robert Cromek. As secretary of the Chalcographic Society, an association of engravers and their supporters, Cromek had proposed a plan to make engravings of twenty famous British paintings. The scheme was to be funded by a group of wealthy connoisseurs at a cost of one hundred pounds each. Blake was well aware that Cromek favored the commercial style of engraving, and it led him to lament that engraving as an art was lost in England.

Blake's was the lament of an artist and craftsman who sees industry and machine methods destroying both art and craft in the interests of business and profit. His plea was for the integrity of the individual artist who unites idea and execution in his work. "Michelangelo's art depends on Michelangelo's execution altogether," he wrote. Once the two are separated, design becomes a matter for a production line, and art is no more than a commodity.

Art is individual and particular, but "Commerce cannot endure Individual Merit." For Blake, art was the highest expression of human freedom. But the machine and its methods enslaved both art and man. "A Machine is not a Man nor a work of Art," he wrote in the *Public Address*. "It is destructive of Humanity and of Art."

Blake's lament was not an isolated case. As the wave of industrialism spread, craftsmen of all kinds were being put out of work, and communal ways of life that had existed for centuries were being overturned. In some communities in the industrial heartland of England, the craftsmen took action, attacking and destroying the machines that had turned their world upside down. Their uprising is known as the Luddite Rebellion.

For a little over a year, the Luddites conducted midnight raids on the factories and workshops that threatened their livelihood and way of life. Most of those involved were framework knitters and hand-loom weavers. It was not that they were opposed to all machines. The hand looms and knitting frames they operated were themselves complex machines, as was the wooden press that Blake printed on. What they and he opposed was the large-scale introduction of machinery that was "hurtful to commonality."

The Luddites were not the first workers to attack machines. "Machine breaking" as a tactic by workers to force owners to settle issues of wages or working hours had a history stretching back over a hundred years. What distinguished the Luddites was that they attacked machines not merely for economic reasons, but also because machines were threatening their entire way of life.

Their rebellion began in the autumn of 1811, in the East Midland county of Nottinghamshire. The harvest had been poor for the third year in a row, the price of bread had skyrocketed, and as a result of the never-ending war with France, the economy was stagnant. Many in the cotton trade were out of work. Now, with the introduction of wide-frame looms that could do the work of many men, the framework knitters and their families grew desperate.

In a series of midnight raids, bands of masked rebels destroyed over eight hundred wide-frame looms. Over the next few months, the movement spread into the neighboring counties of Lancashire, Derbyshire, Leicestershire, and north into Yorkshire. In alarm, the government sent troops from London to quash the rebellion.

But the rebels were not easily put down. They operated as widely scattered bands of twenty to forty men. They swore oaths of secrecy, worked only by night, and faded invisibly back into their communities. Each of the bands was under the leadership of one they called General Ludd. There were perhaps a hundred General Ludds. He was everywhere, yet nowhere. The name had come from the story of a boy named Ned Ludd, an apprentice knitter who had been

Rawfold's textile mill, Yorkshire – the first to be entirely mechanized. Scene of the disastrous Luddite raid of April 1812.

beaten by his master for not working hard enough. The boy took a hammer and destroyed the master's knitting machine. Taking action against a machine became known as "Ned Ludding" it.

The Luddites went out of their way to avoid violence against people. Their targets were machines, housed for the most part in small workshops, but increasingly in new, heavily fortified factories or mills. In the early months of 1812, several such mills were attacked successfully and their machines destroyed, with no loss of life. By April, all that was to change.

Rawfold's Mill stood in the heart of West Yorkshire. It was four stories high and more than sixty feet long. The owner, William Cartwright, anticipating Luddite troubles, had taken to sleeping in the mill to guard the fifty new wool-finishing machines he had hauled there across the moors.

On the night of April 12, 1812, several bands of Luddite rebels, many of them Yorkshire wool "croppers" put out of work by the new machines, met on the moors and marched against Rawfold's Mill. There were over two hundred rebels, and this was their largest raid yet. They had no hint of what lay in store.

Cartwright had company in his mill that night – four heavily armed guards and five local militia. As the rebels tried to break down the door, they were fired upon from inside. Two were seriously wounded and later died in custody; the others, many of them wounded, fled into the night. At least two of these also died of their wounds. It was a major defeat. Two weeks later, a local factory owner, William Horsfall, was killed in reprisal. This marked the beginning of the end.

The government poured more troops into the area – over fourteen thousand, one of the largest forces ever sent by England against its own citizens. It passed new laws, making machine breaking a capital crime, punishable by hanging. With the aid of spies and paid informants, those involved in the raid on Rawfold's Mill and the death of William Horsfall were brought to trial. Many of the convicted were sentenced to be transported to Australia, others to be hanged. On January 16, 1813, at York Castle in Yorkshire, fourteen men were hanged at a public execution. Their deaths effectively marked the end of the Luddite Rebellion.

In the summer of 1810, Blake's public exhibition came to a close. The only review of the exhibit came from Robert Hunt of *The Examiner*, who had savaged *The Grave* when it appeared and now continued his personal attack on Blake:

> an unfortunate lunatic whose personal inoffensiveness secures him from confinement. . . . the poor man fancies himself a great master, and has painted a few wretched pictures, some of which are unintelligible allegory, others an attempt at sober character by caricature representation, and the whole "blotted and blurred" and very badly drawn. These

he calls an Exhibition, of which he has published a Catalogue, or rather a farrago of nonsense, unintelligibleness and egregious vanity, the wild effusions of a distempered brain.

And so, with his "Character both as an artist and a Man . . . blasted," Blake's bid to win public recognition for his paintings came to an end. By all material standards, it was a failure. Yet he had had his say, in his own way and on his own terms.

In October, he published his engraving of the Canterbury Pilgrims. Though it is one of the finest engravings he ever produced, he lacked Cromek's ability to attract public interest, and sales were modest.

Blake had failed, but he was not defeated:

If a man is master at his profession, he cannot be ignorant that he is so; and if he is not employed by those who pretend to encourage art, he will employ himself, and laugh in secret at the pretences of the ignorant, while he has every night dropped into his shoe, as soon as he puts it off, and puts out the candle, and gets into bed, a reward for the labours of the day, such as the world cannot give, and patience and time await to give him all that the world can give.

On this resigned note, Blake concluded his *Descriptive Catalogue* and put a period of turmoil and bitter disappointment behind him. For the next several years he led a hidden life, far from the fray of engraving and publishing, far from the competitive realm of commerce and the fragmented world of the machine.

For the sake of his freedom and independence, he abandoned it all and accepted poverty as his lot. To the world, it seemed he had died. But, in fact, he had only gone on pilgrimage. He was traveling toward that city of freedom and joy he called *Jerusalem*.

CHAPTER TWELVE

THE HIDDEN YEARS

DOES THY GOD, O PRIEST,
TAKE SUCH VENGEANCE AS THIS?

OR THE NEXT SEVERAL YEARS, BLAKE DROPPED ALMOST completely out of sight. There are no commercial engravings from this period, no letters, few sightings. He and Catherine settled into a life of quiet obscurity at 17 South Molton Street. Their habits were simple, their wants were few, and they were content in one another's company.

> I rose up at the dawn of day –
> Get thee away! Get thee away!
> Pray'st thou for Riches? away! away!
> This is the Throne of Mammon grey.

Said I, "this sure is very odd.
"I took it to be the Throne of God.
"For every Thing besides I have:
"It is only for Riches that I can crave.

"I have Mental Joy and Mental Health
"And Mental Friends & Mental Wealth;
"I've a Wife I love & that loves me;
"I've all But Riches Bodily.

"I am in God's presence night & day,
"And he never turns his face away.
"The accuser of sins by my side does stand
"And he holds my money bag in his hand. . . .

"He says, if I do not worship him for a God,
"I shall eat coarser food & go worse shod;
"So as I don't value such things as these,
"You must do, Mr. devil, just as God please."

It would be wrong to paint this as a period of despair and distress. The evidence is, rather, that during these "hidden" years, William and Catherine grew in love and harmony. There had been storms; there had been bitterness and heartbreak; but now, despite material hardship, there was spiritual peace.

Throughout these years, Blake kept up his friendship with Thomas Butts. He continued to paint for him, though not on the same scale that he once had. The Buttses' house was now full of Blake's work and remained the chief repository for his paintings for many years. Still, from 1811 to 1820, Butts purchased over thirty more of Blake's paintings, many of them illustrating poems by Milton.

These occasional commissions brought in much-needed money. Blake also earned a little by teaching. Butts's son Tommy, who had been an engraving

Pencil portrait of Catherine Blake by Blake, c. 1805, drawn on the back of a page from Hayley's Ballads. *You can see the show-through of the type.*

student of his for many years, continued to visit the Blakes at South Molton Street, sometimes with his friend Seymour Kirkup. Kirkup was an art student at the Royal Academy, and the Butts family tried to interest him in studying under Blake. Years later, he wrote, "I was ignorant enough to think him mad at the time and neglected sadly the opportunities the Buttses threw my way."

Somehow William and Catherine managed to get by. Catherine put together their frugal meals, made and mended their clothes, and managed their meager resources. Over the years she had learned that talk of money only led to friction. "Were I to love money, I should lose all power of original thought," Blake once said. "Desire of gain deadens the genius in man. My business is not to gather gold, but to make glorious shapes."

Rather than squabble over money, Catherine simply set before her husband at dinner whatever there was to eat in the house, without comment. Finally, when she placed an empty plate before him, Blake was reminded that it was time to make a little money. Yet, even when things were at their worst, Catherine always managed to keep a little bit tucked away for emergencies.

Time and need had altered the two of them. Their clothes were common and often dirty. A friend who saw Catherine after a lapse of years said he never saw a woman so changed. But to William, who looked with the eyes of love, she was always the pretty girl with the gleaming black eyes he had met those many years ago in Battersea.

Catherine believed in his visions. Indeed, she shared in them so much that their friend George Cumberland once remarked, "She is the maddest of the two." They were utterly devoted to one another, and despite the hardships the world threw their way, they went on and on.

The rift with Flaxman over *The Grave* mended in time. In 1814 he secured for Blake the commission to engrave thirty-seven plates from Flaxman's drawings to Hesiod's *Works and Days* and *Theogony*. It was a large and a lucrative undertaking. Flaxman was also preparing an article on sculpture for Rees's *Cyclopaedia*, and Blake was commissioned to make engravings of a number of famous statues to illustrate it.

Wedgwood Ware, 1817. Some of Blake's engravings for a salesman's catalogue.

As part of this project, William visited the Royal Academy to make sketches of the *Laocoon* from the full-size cast of the original there. While he was sketching with a group of students, his old friend Henry Fuseli, now the Keeper of the Academy, came up to him where he sat on a low stool at the foot of the statue and said, "What! You here, Mister Blake? We ought to come and learn of you, not you of us." Blake took his friend's kind remark with simple joy.

In addition to these two commissions, Flaxman was also responsible for sending work of a humbler nature Blake's way. He introduced him to the pottery manufacturer Josiah Wedgwood (the younger). Flaxman had been making designs for the Wedgwood firm for many years. Blake was to make engravings for the salesmen's catalogues. Samples of soup tureens, butter boats, and cream bowls were sent to South Molton Street for Blake to sketch. He would send the finished drawings off to Wedgwood for approval, and then be sent another shipment of pottery to draw. In the end, Blake made 189 small engravings from his drawings, arranged on eighteen copper plates, and was paid a modest thirty pounds.

At about this time, Blake was invited to a party hosted by Lady Caroline Lamb. The incident is recorded in the diary of Lady Charlotte Bury:

She had collected a strange party of artists and literati. . . . Sir T[homas] Lawrence, next whom I sat at dinner, is as courtly as ever. . . . Then there was another eccentric little artist, by name Blake; not a regular professional painter, but one of those persons who follow the art for its own sweet sake, and derive their happiness from its pursuit. He appeared to me full of beautiful imaginations and genius; but how far the execution of his designs is equal to the conceptions of his mental vision, I know not, never having seen them. . . . He looks care-worn and subdued; but his countenance radiated as he spoke of his favourite pursuit, and he appeared gratified by talking to a person who comprehended his feelings. I can easily imagine that he seldom meets with any one who enters into his views; for they are peculiar and exalted above the common level of

Lady Charlotte Bury recorded her meeting with Blake at a party in 1818. She was famous for the court diary she kept while lady-in-waiting to the future Queen Caroline. As a young woman, she was noted for her beauty, as seen here in this early portrait.

received opinions. . . . Sir T. Lawrence looked at me several times whilst I was talking with Mr. B., and I saw his lips curl with a sneer. . . . It was very evident that Sir Thomas did not like the company he found himself in.

"They pity me," Blake said of prosperous society artists like Sir Thomas, "but tis they are the just objects of pity: I possess my visions and my peace. They have bartered their birthright for a mess of Pottage."

Throughout these hidden years, Blake was working on the last and the longest of his Illuminated Books, *Jerusalem*. It comprises one hundred closely written, richly illuminated plates and is his crowning achievement in Illuminated Printing.

In rejecting the ways of the world of commerce and the spread of machine methods into the world of art, Blake embraced the Illuminated Book with renewed passion. While industrial production prided itself on the ability to make an endless stream of identical copies, in Illuminated Printing each copy was unique. While industry prided itself on speed and efficiency, Blake's mode of production was deliberately slow and inefficient. While industrial production was grounded on the division of labor and the distinction between those who worked with their heads and those who worked with their hands, Blake's was an artisan's spirit. He took pride in the work of his hands and relentlessly pursued the unity of head and hands in the work of art. With the Illuminated Book, Blake strove to restore writing to the "wondrous art" it was.

By devoting himself to this deliberately small, deliberately slow, deliberately primitive mode of production, Blake was turning his back on the world of the machine and all that followed from it.

On the opening page of *Jerusalem*, there is a picture of the hero of the poem – a poet in the image of Blake himself, down to the broad-brimmed hat he wore – turning away from us as he steps through an arched doorway into the dark. Blake names this character Los, an anagram of the Latin word for "sun" – *sol*. In fact, he carries a globe of fire like the sun to light his way as he enters the inner world.

> . . . I rest not from my great task!
> To open the Eternal Worlds, to open the immortal Eyes
> Of Man inwards into the Worlds of Thought, into Eternity
> Ever expanding in the Bosom of God, the Human Imagination.

Jerusalem is the record of this journey inward, a journey from death to life, from sleep to awakening. It opens in a lifeless "land of snares & traps & wheels

Jerusalem *frontispiece, plate 1, Los with his globe of fire searches the interiors of Albion's Bosom. Blake worked on the poem for sixteen years.*

& pit-falls & dire mills," an image of the bleak industrial landscape of Blake's England. The giant Albion (the Latin name for England) has fallen from his former glory. For most of the poem he lies in a deadly sleep, stretched out on a rock in the sea, like England herself.

> Albion cold lays on his Rock: storms & snows beat round him . . .
> Howling winds cover him: roaring seas dash furious against him:
> In the deep darkness broad lightnings glare, long thunders roll.

It is up to the poet Los, Albion's power of imagination, to attempt to awaken him from his deadly sleep.

Los's journey, as he takes up his globe of fire "to search the interiors of Albion's Bosom," is Blake's own as he walks the streets of London by night. He sees the poverty and suffering of young and old, "the jewels of Albion running down the kennels of the streets & lanes as if they were abhorr'd . . . and all the tendernesses of the soul cast forth as filth and mire."

It is Los's task to defend these little ones, for no matter how small or poor or mean they may appear on the outside, each one is "translucent all within" and is holy. This is the divine vision that Los keeps "in time of trouble," until Albion at last awakes.

And when he does, all creation wakes with him. The coverings that enclose each living thing are broken; the veils that divide one from another fall away; and each individual is free to give forth "its own peculiar Light."

> And now the time returns again:
> Our souls exult, & London's towers
> Receive the Lamb of God to dwell
> In England's green & pleasant bowers.

And what has ushered in this new world? Forgiveness. Blake had come to see that without forgiveness, the "Mysterious offering of Self for Another,"

Jerusalem, *title page, plate 2, "O lovely*
mild Jerusalem, Wing'd with Six Wings."

friendship and brotherhood could not be. And without "Friendship and Brotherhood . . . Man Is Not." If we do not forgive the wrongs we have done one another, we are imprisoned in anger and selfhood, and the cycle of vengeance is unending.

At about this time, Blake took out the plates for the little emblem book he had published over twenty years before. He added a motto to the title page, which begins with the lines, "Mutual Forgiveness of each Vice/ Such are the Gates of Paradise."

There on the frontispiece of *The Gates of Paradise* is the child wound in its cocoon, asleep on the oak leaf. Like Albion asleep on his rock, this child is called to "wake! expand!" For "in every bosom a Universe expands as wings."

On the title page of *Jerusalem*, we see Jerusalem herself, the symbol of liberty and creative vision, lying in the same position as the child, but freed now of the confining shell, her wings unfurled, patterned with sun and moon and stars, a universe expanding as wings.

Jerusalem ends in a vision of the world redeemed by mutual forgiveness, which in turn releases the creative power harbored in each creature. It is a vision of unity in infinite variety, of the joyous life of the imagination opening in and through all things. It is a vision of Innocence that returns us to the world of *Songs of Innocence.*

So the vast labor of the Illuminated Books, in the end, brings us back to the beginning, and the vision that inspired that first book is the same vision that concludes the last.

As in art, so in life. Blake's heart went out to the poor and the oppressed, those for whom life was an endless struggle. His own life had its share of bitter disappointment and heartbreak. He came to believe that struggle was the very essence of life, and his work is full of it. What separates Blake's story from many others is that he was sustained throughout his struggle by vision, a vision of unity and harmony and joy that he had tasted in his own life and saw in the lives of children and the lowly of the earth. If his life may be said to describe a pattern, it is the very pattern he saw operating in and through all things: a state of initial bliss, followed by a fall into darkness and strife, and then, finally, a restoration to unity and peace.

It is the refrain of all his poetry and the sustaining vision of his life. In *Songs of Innocence,* he celebrated the vision of joy. In *Songs of Experience* and many of the books that followed, he sang of division, constraint, and darkness. Yet even in times of trouble, he kept the divine vision. He had known bliss, known darkness and strife. In the final years of his life, he would experience a return to the world of light, to the joys of friendship and creative fellowship, and the visionary company of children.

CHAPTER THIRTEEN

VISIONS AND VIRGIL

FEAR & HOPE ARE — VISION

T BEGAN IN THE SUMMER OF 1818, WHEN GEORGE CUMBERLAND Jr. brought around a friend of his to meet Blake. That friend was the twenty-six-year-old John Linnell, an up-and-coming artist who had been giving lessons in landscape painting to Cumberland. It was a momentous meeting, for in John Linnell, Blake was to find both a devoted friend and a generous patron in the last years of his life.

The two got on well from the beginning. Linnell, also, was a Londoner, the son of a frame-maker and picture dealer. He had shown a gift for drawing from an early age. By the time he was ten, he was sketching portraits and copying the watercolors of popular artists for his father to sell in his shop. Like the young Blake, he, too, used to hang about the auction houses, and he had a fine collection of engravings. An ardent admirer of Michelangelo and Dürer, he had studied at the Royal Academy under Fuseli.

Linnell was a man of strong religious beliefs, a Dissenter with a distinctly puritan cast about him. During the time he knew Blake, he worshipped with the Baptists, but he had also considered joining the Quakers. In later life he stood apart from all sects, yet retained his religious zeal.

At many points, then, their characters and experiences were in harmony. Despite the gulf of years between them, for Blake was now nearly sixty-one, they quickly became friends. It was apparent to Linnell from the start that Blake was in need, "having scarcely enough employment to live by at the prices he could obtain."

Immediately he brought some work Blake's way. A talented engraver in his own right, Linnell had been asked to make an engraving from a portrait he had painted of a Baptist minister, Mr. Upton. He commissioned Blake to lay in the outlines for him and then to pass the plate back to him for the finishing. For his work, Blake was paid fifteen pounds. He delivered the plate to Linnell on September 12, just four days after the birth of the Linnells' first child, Hannah.

The two men began to socialize regularly. They visited art exhibitions, went to the theater, and paid calls on Linnell's circle of friends. Blake was welcomed with open arms into the Linnell family. In his notebook are three small sketches of a baby's face dating from this period – likely the infant Hannah. The sudden presence of children in Blake's life, and the attentions of a gifted young artist, proved inspirational. In the months following their meeting, for the first time in several years, Blake began to print copies of his early work. He made new copies of *Songs of Innocence* and *Songs of Experience*, coloring them with the care of works of art. Linnell purchased a set at a special price, and it was from Blake's *Songs* that young Hannah learned her letters.

Linnell was not blind to Blake's eccentricities and admitted to being "somewhat taken aback by the boldness of some of his assertions." But he found that if he did not mock those views, or oppose them as many did, Blake was more than ready to explain his opinions in a friendly manner.

William Blake, a portrait by John Linnell, 1820.

Other artists were among the circle of friends to whom Linnell introduced Blake, some of them rather odd in their own right. One was Linnell's former teacher, John Varley. Like Blake, Linnell had never gone to school, but from the age of twelve, he had boarded with Varley at his home on Broad Street, just a few doors down from the Blake family home, and been taught the art of painting. In addition to being a fine teacher, Varley was a gifted watercolorist.

Full of a seemingly boundless energy, he was generous to a fault. Because of his generosity to his needy friends and fellow artists, he often found himself in financial difficulties and was several times imprisoned for debt. He would take his art materials to prison with him and paint until he had paid the debt off.

Varley was supremely unlucky. Three times his house burned to the ground, along with all his possessions. Yet he remained a man of high spirits. "All these troubles are necessary to me," he once told Linnell. "If it were not for my troubles I should burst with joy."

On a par with his passion for painting stood his fervor for palmistry and astrology. He crammed all his astrological charts and almanacs into the enormous pockets of his old-fashioned tailcoat. Whenever he met someone, the first thing he would ask was the time and place of his birth. And he would immediately make elaborate mathematical calculations and cast his horoscope.

His predictions were remarkably accurate. On one occasion, he cast the horoscope of the artist A.W. Calcott and sealed it in an envelope that was not opened for many years. He had predicted that the artist would remain single until he was fifty, then marry and move to Italy. All these things had in fact occurred.

Each morning, Varley would cast his horoscope for the day. Once, on doing so, he realized he was under the evil influence of the recently discovered planet Uranus and would suffer some misfortune before noon. As the hour approached, he became more and more agitated. Shortly before noon, he said to his son, "I am feeling all right: I do not think anything is going to happen to me personally; it must be my property that is threatened."

At that precise moment, there was a cry of "Fire!" Varley rushed outside with his son and discovered that his house was on fire. He was so delighted that his prediction had proved true that he sat down and promptly wrote an account of his discovery of the astrological influence of Uranus, while his house burned to the ground.

When he met Blake, Varley was immediately drawn to the artist's visionary gifts. Blake's claim to have continuous communion with the spirit world fired Varley's imagination. As Linnell wryly noted, "Varley believed in the reality of Blake's visions more than even Blake himself." And so came to pass one of the more curious episodes in Blake's life – the drawing of the Visionary Heads.

Blake had long been in the habit of speaking matter-of-factly of his spiritual visitors. One day, Varley suggested that he draw their portraits while they were with him. And so, beginning in the autumn of 1819, Blake would regularly visit Varley's house from nine in the evening until well after midnight, and make portraits of the spirits who appeared to him.

At times Varley would request the portrait of some historical figure, such as King David or Moses or Julius Caesar. At other times a spirit would appear unsummoned. There would often be long delays, and Varley would doze off, only to be startled by Blake's sudden cry of "There he is!" as he snatched up his pencil and hastily sketched the supernatural visitor in the notebook Varley had given him.

All the while, Varley would be staring with all his might, hoping to catch a glimpse of the invisible presence. When Blake had finished his sketch, he would hand the portrait to Varley, who would carefully note the name of the visitant and the exact time of its appearance. It is an odd and fascinating list, including Edward the First, Richard *Coeur de Lion*, The Man who built the Pyramids, Colonel Blood, Bathsheba, and The Man who instructed Mr. Blake in Painting in his Dreams.

In some measure, Blake may have simply indulged his friend's fancy in all this. The literal-minded Varley looked on Blake as a sort of medium, summoning

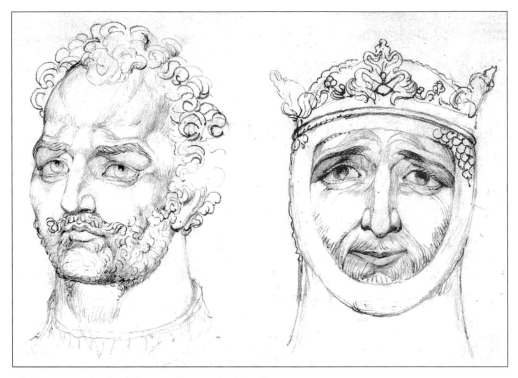

Visionary Heads of William Wallace and Edward I, 1819.

spirits to a seance. But for Blake, these spirits were the product of imagination worked up into a state of vision, a power he claimed everyone possessed, though few exercised it.

One evening Varley called on Blake, who told him he had just seen a most remarkable vision – the Ghost of a Flea. Varley sat down and urged him to draw it, should it return. A short time later, the vision reappeared. "Reach me my things," said Blake, "while I keep an eye on him." And he proceeded to draw a portrait in profile of a malevolent creature, its skin scaled, its tongue flicking from its mouth.

Later, he painted a tempera of the horrific vision, perhaps in part an echo of the grim figure he had seen striding down the stairs toward him those many years ago in Lambeth. The creature in the painting is caught walking across a

The Ghost of a Flea, *c. 1819, "holding a bloody cup in its clawed hands out of which it seems eager to drink."*

doorway whose curtain has been drawn back to reveal a night sky flecked with stars, cut across with a blazing comet. It is covered in green and gold scales. Half-human, half-insect, it peers greedily down into the bleeding-bowl it holds in one hand, while the other hand clutches a knife.

It is a superb symbolic picture, showing the blood lust of a murderous human spirit inhabiting the body of a flea.

In the fall of 1818, Blake met Dr. Robert Thornton, a physician and noted botanist. Thornton was the Linnells' family doctor. Over the years, he had published several lavishly illustrated books on botany – projects that had almost impoverished him. But he had also published a textbook of Virgil's *Pastorals* adapted for use in schools, which had done quite well and was about to enter its third edition.

Thornton planned to make substantial additions to the illustrations for this new edition, and he commissioned both Blake and Linnell to work on the project. Blake was to execute twenty-seven engravings, seven of which were to be regular copper engravings of famous figures, and the remaining twenty to be small original designs to accompany the text. For economy, these small designs were to be engraved on wood so they could be printed simultaneously with the type.

There was one problem. Blake had never engraved on wood before. He decided to try the method of relief etching he had discovered and used in his Illuminated Books, as it produced a design that was printed in much the same way as a wood engraving.

Setting to work, he composed directly on the copper, as was his habit, casting Virgil's pastoral vision in an idealized English landscape.

At some point, he must have shown his work to Thornton, who was likely taken aback by Blake's unconventional designs. There may have also been a problem in properly inking the relief etchings to print alongside the typeset

Four woodcuts from
Thornton's Virgil, *1821,*
"visions of little dells and
nooks and corners of
Paradise."

text and the more conventional wood block engravings. Whatever the reason, Blake was forced to abandon the scheme and begin again.

The engravings were to be printed four to the page and were, therefore, quite small, roughly 1½" × 3". He drew his designs first on paper, then transferred them to wood blocks. The images were full of mood and power, but looked raw and primitive, lacking the smooth mechanical finish that appealed to popular taste.

When Thornton saw the finished engravings, he was shocked. The printers echoed his sentiments. "This will never do," they said, and immediately ordered the blocks to be recut by one of their regular engravers. By the time Linnell visited Thornton with Blake to sort the matter out, three of the designs had already been recut by a journeyman engraver in a more acceptable style.

The rest would surely have suffered the same fate had Thornton not happened to attend a dinner party at the home of collector Charles Aders, where a number of well-respected artists were present, including Linnell, James Ward, and Sir Thomas Lawrence.

The conversation turned to Blake's designs for Thornton's *Virgil*. To Thornton's amazement, all the artists around the table expressed their admiration for Blake's woodcuts and pleaded that they be saved. Though unconvinced, Thornton was persuaded to change his mind. The remaining seventeen blocks were printed, though they suffered the indignity of being pared down to fit the page better.

In the published book, Thornton could not resist prefacing Blake's unorthodox designs with an apology:

The Illustrations of this English Pastoral are by the famous BLAKE, the illustrator of Young's *Night Thoughts* and Blair's *Grave*; who designed and engraved them himself. This is mentioned, as they display less of art than genius, and are much admired by some eminent painters.

Following his bitter experience with Robert Cromek and *The Grave*, Blake had made no commercial book engravings from his own designs until he worked on these woodcuts. This time around the fates looked more kindly on him. For while the seventeen tiny wood engravings went mostly unnoticed by his contemporaries, it was these among all his works that were to have the most profound impact on the small band of eager young artists who were soon to enter his life.

CHAPTER FOURTEEN

TWO SMALL ROOMS IN FOUNTAIN COURT

THE TRAVELLER HASTETH
IN THE EVENING

 N 1821, AFTER SEVENTEEN YEARS OF LIVING AT SOUTH MOLTON Street, the Blakes moved. Their landlord had retired from business and emigrated to France. William and Catherine found new lodgings at Number 3 Fountain Court, The Strand, a house owned by Catherine's brother-in-law, Henry Banes. The rent may have been more reasonable because of that, but it was a step down.

Fountain Court was an area of warehouses and private dwellings lying near the end of a dark narrow lane leading south from The Strand to the muddy banks of the river. The Blakes' two rooms on the second floor were small and dim. The front room faced east and overlooked the court. Here they set up their

Number 3 Fountain Court, Blake's final residence.

wooden press and hung the walls with William's pictures. A door opened off this onto the back room, which served as kitchen, workroom, and bedroom. They settled their few sticks of furniture here. William placed his worktable by the window, where he could look down a narrow gap between Fountain Court and the neighboring street and catch a glimpse of the Thames and the Surrey hills beyond. He remembered how, as a boy, he had delighted in wandering there. "I live in a hole here," he would say, "but God has a beautiful mansion for me elsewhere."

The move put a strain on their meager finances, and shortly afterward, Blake was forced to sell off his large collection of old prints.

When John Linnell became aware of Blake's financial straits, he sought money from the Royal Academy on his behalf, stating that Blake was "labouring under great distress." The application was approved, and the Academy sent a donation of twenty-five pounds through him to Blake. It was, at best, a temporary measure.

Meanwhile, Linnell continued to introduce William to his circle of friends, with the intent of seeking patronage for the struggling artist. At one of the dinner parties they attended, the beautiful young daughter of one of the guests was introduced to Blake. He looked kindly at the child and, stroking her long ringlets, said, "May God make this world to you, my child, as beautiful as it has been to me."

About this time, Blake may have taken Linnell to visit his old friend and patron Thomas Butts to show him the vast collection of his paintings that filled the walls of Butts's large house in Fitzroy Square. Among these was a series of watercolor illustrations to the Book of Job, which he had painted for Butts some fifteen years earlier. Linnell was struck by the power and beauty of these paintings and commissioned a set for himself.

Despite Linnell's best intentions, however, Blake's situation remained precarious. By now, Blake was in the habit of dining with the Linnells on Sundays. On one such occasion, in discussing ways of finding Blake some project that could ease his situation, Linnell suggested that Blake do a series of engravings based on the Job watercolors. They could bind them up as a book and attempt to sell it. Like *The Gates of Paradise*, it would be a sort of emblem book, with only a minimal amount of text.

A formal agreement was drawn up between them on March 25, 1823:

> W. Blake agrees to Engrave the Set of Plates from his own Designs of Job's Captivity in number twenty, for John Linnell – and John Linnell agrees to pay William Blake five Pounds pr. Plate or one hundred Pounds for the set part before and the remainder when the Plates are finished, as Mr. Blake may require it, besides which J. Linnell agrees to give W. Blake one hundred pounds more out of the Profits of the work as the receipts will admit of it.
>
>   Signed J. Linnell   Willm. Blake
>
> N.B. J.L. to find Copper Plates.

Five pounds per plate was not a large amount, but it was what Linnell could afford, and there was the promise of future profits if the book sold well. The arrangement offered Blake two significant things: a steady income, for it became his habit to generally draw a pound or two a week from Linnell; and, more importantly, the freedom to engrave again from his own designs.

He began by making reduced drawings from the watercolor series he had copied for Linnell. He bound these up in a small book and used them as models as he composed the designs on the copper plate in pencil or chalk and began to cut them with the graver.

On his weekly visits to Linnell, Blake would take along the plate he was working on, to show Linnell his progress and to ask for his comments and suggestions. Not only was Linnell able to offer his own expertise, he also directed Blake to the work of the early Italian engravers Bonasone and Marcantonio.

The entire project reflected the liberating influence of Linnell on Blake's technique. Blake cut his lines as cleanly as ever, but there was a newfound freedom and flexibility in those lines, as if he were drawing on the plate with

Illustrations of the Book of Job, *plate 1*, Thus did Job continually, *1826*.

the graver. In these late works, he abandoned the mixed method technique he had been trained in and worked entirely with the graver with no preliminary etching of the plate.

The twenty-two plates that make up the *Illustrations of the Book of Job* stand at the summit of Blake's art as an engraver. He worked on them for close to three years. The story they tell echoes the grand theme that ran through both his work and his life – our suffering and spiritual death at the hands of our Selfhood, and the final joyful recovery of the inward God, the creative Imagination. It is the Book of Job read in the spiritual sense.

The opening plate presents a picture of Job in prosperity, surrounded by his

Illustrations of the Book of Job, *plate 21,* So the Lord blessed the latter end of Job more than the beginning, *1826.*

wife and children and his flocks of sheep. The family is at prayer. Job and his wife sit side by side beneath the tree, their holy books open on their laps, their children kneeling to either side.

It seems a picture of perfect peace. But if we look closer, we see that all is not well. In the text below the illustration are the words, "The Letter Killeth, the Spirit giveth Life." This suggests that Job's piety relies on passively obeying a code of law written in books rather than on the exercise of the spiritual gifts each of us possesses. That explains why the musical instruments are hanging idle in the branches of the tree.

The sun is setting, and the night is coming on. The plates that follow portray the sufferings of Job at the hands of Satan before the final revelation of the true God, who dwells within him.

The final plate in the series is paired with the first. The long night is over and a new day is dawning. Job and his wife and family are reunited beneath the tree. But now they have taken down the musical instruments that hung in the branches, and with music and song give praise to God in joyful harmony.

This was a blissful period in Blake's life. Not only was he free to work on the story of Job, which had occupied his mind for many years, but he was also able to express it with the tools of the craft in which he had been trained in his youth.

One day in the spring of 1824, Linnell brought around a young artist friend to meet Blake. That friend was Samuel Palmer, and the meeting had a lasting impact on him. Years later, he recalled:

> At my never-to-be-forgotten first interview the copper of the first plate – "Thus did Job continually" – was lying on the table where he had been working on it. How lovely it looked by the lamplight, strained through the tissue paper.

Shortly after this, Palmer visited Blake again, this time bringing along some of his own designs. He found the aging artist confined to bed with a scalded leg. The bed was covered in books, and Blake, unable to sit at his table to engrave the Job plates, was working instead on the designs for a series of drawings to Dante's *Divine Comedy*, which was to be his next commission for Linnell. He said he had begun them with fear and trembling.

"Oh! I have enough of fear and trembling," said Palmer.

"Then, you'll do," said Blake.

Palmer showed Blake some of the drawings he had brought along with him:

Samuel Palmer, self-portrait,
1826. Palmer was the most
devoted of the Ancients. He would
kiss the bell-handle in homage
before entering Blake's house in
Fountain Court.

and the sweet encouragement he gave me . . . made me work harder and better that afternoon and night. And, after visiting him, the scene recurs to me afterwards in a kind of vision; . . . my spirit sees his dwelling . . . as it were an island in the midst of the sea – such a place for primitive grandeur, whether in the persons of Mr. and Mrs. Blake, or in the things hanging on the walls.

Palmer spread the news of Blake among his circle of friends – young artists like himself, who called themselves the Ancients. Ancient they were not. Edward Calvert, the eldest of the group, was twenty-five, while George Richmond, the youngest, was just fifteen. The others included Frederick Tatham and his brother Arthur, Francis Finch, Welby Sherman, and John Giles.

The Ancients held monthly meetings, read poetry together, went on excursions into the countryside around Shoreham, and painted there in the open air. They congregated at a run-down cottage Palmer had purchased in the area, which he called Rat Abbey.

They took their name from their belief that ancient man was superior to modern man. They embraced the ancient ideals of art and saw in Blake an example of one who lived wholly for art's sake. "Never have I known an artist so spiritual, so devoted, so single-minded, or cherishing imagination as he did," wrote George Richmond.

The Ancients began to visit Blake frequently at Fountain Court. They referred to it as "the House of the Interpreter," after a scene in *The Pilgrim's Progress* in which Christian, on his way to Mount Zion from the City of Destruction, arrives at the House of the Interpreter and says to him, "I was told . . . that if I called here, you would show me excellent things, such as would be an help to me in my Journey."

Among the excellent things Blake was able to show them were his woodcuts to Thornton's *Virgil*. To his older contemporaries these designs had appeared crude, but to these young men they embodied the very spirit of art. "They are visions of little dells, and nooks, and corners of Paradise; models of the exquisitest pitch of intense poetry," wrote Palmer, many years later.

Blake opened his mind fully to these young men. A bond of sympathy existed between them. He spoke of his own youth, of his visions, and of art and imagination. He was always ready to help them with their own art, or to offer them support at those times when inspiration failed.

George Richmond visited once while the Blakes were sitting at tea. He told Blake he felt his power to create had deserted him. Blake turned to Catherine and said, "It is just so with us, is it not, for weeks together when the visions forsake us? What do we do then, Kate?"

"We kneel down and pray, Mr. Blake."

One day Blake went with Samuel Palmer to see an exhibit at the Royal Academy. At home, the clothes he commonly wore were threadbare, but on occasions such as this he put on his best, if rather old-fashioned, clothes – black knee breeches, black stockings, thick shoes with ties, a frock coat, and a broad-brimmed Quakerish hat.

As Palmer stood with him, quietly examining the pictures on display while the fashionable in all their finery milled about them, he thought, "How little you know *who* is among you."

The Ancients were certainly not blind to Blake's poverty, but where others might have seen "everything in the room squalid and . . . offensive," as Henry Crabb Robinson had when he visited Blake about this time, they saw in Blake one who "ennobled poverty, and, by his conversation and the influence of his genius, made two small rooms in Fountain Court more attractive than the threshold of princes."

And so, with this sudden wealth of friends and kindred spirits, Blake continued to work on the Job engravings. He sat at the window, facing the light as he worked, and from time to time would glance down the gap between the houses and catch a glimpse of the Thames, gleaming in the distance "like a bar of gold."

From the courtyard below came the sound of children at play. Once, leading a friend to the window, he pointed down at them and said, "That is heaven."

CHAPTER FIFTEEN

HAMPSTEAD: FINAL DAYS

DEATH'S DOOR

 N MARCH 1824, JOHN LINNELL AND HIS FAMILY MOVED FROM their London home to Collins' Farm in Hampstead, a suburb north of the city. The cottage lay tucked in a hollow, just beyond Hampstead Heath. The front faced south and looked upon the heather-clad hills of the heath, while the rear overlooked meadows and hedgerows. The Linnell family had been spending their summers in this rural setting for the previous two years, before deciding to move there year-round. Linnell kept their London house in Cirencester Place as a studio.

On Sundays, if the weather was good, Blake would make the trek to Hampstead to dine with the Linnells. He would often stop in Broad Street on the way to pick up Samuel Palmer, who would accompany him. He and young

William Blake at Hampstead *by John Linnell, 1825, in his frock coat and "Quakerish" hat.*

John Linnell *at
Hampstead, inscribed by
Linnell, "Drawn by Mr.
Blake from the life, 1825."*

Palmer would make their way northward through the city toward the high ground of the heath. Soon city gave way to countryside; cobbled streets to leafy, winding lanes. It was like the country rambles he had delighted in as a boy. Walking along with young Palmer, he would share those boyhood memories.

"To walk with him in the country," recalled Palmer, many years later, "was to perceive the soul of beauty through the forms of matter." Palmer remained profoundly moved by the primitive beauty of the countryside all his life. It seemed a vision of the spiritual world glimpsed through the glass of Nature.

Blake often carried a sketchbook along with him, for he was in the habit of giving Mrs. Linnell a drawing lesson when he visited on Sundays. He would wrap the Job plate he was working on carefully in tissue paper and tuck it between the leaves of the book so that he might show it to Linnell.

The Linnell children eagerly looked forward to Blake's visits. Six-year-old Hannah and her younger brother and sister would watch at the window for his arrival. And when he appeared with Palmer over the crest of the hill, he would signal to them in a special way, and they would hurry out to meet him.

Often there were other visitors – John Varley, Dr. Thornton, and other family friends. The conversation over dinner was animated, and though she often did not understand what he was saying, young Hannah was fascinated by the grave, sedate old gentleman with his large bright eyes, who spoke in his quiet, kindly way of the most remarkable things.

"The other evening I was out taking a walk," said Blake, on an earlier occasion. "I came to a meadow, and at the far corner of it there was a fold of lambs. The ground blushed with flowers, and the sheep lying in their shelter of woven branches made a beautiful pastoral scene. Yet as I came nearer, I saw that it was no living flock, but beautiful sculpture."

"I beg your pardon, Mr. Blake," said one of the guests, eager to see the scene herself, "but may I ask *where* you saw this?"

"Here, madam," said Blake, touching his forehead.

Sometimes after dinner, Mrs. Linnell would sit at the piano and sing old Scottish songs, and the tears would well up in Blake's eyes. He would take the children on his knee and sing to them from *Songs of Innocence* to tunes of his own making, and tell them stories of the spiritual things that were so real to him and so near.

Once, seeing Hannah busily trying to draw a face, he took the pencil and showed her, with a few quick strokes, how to give it the look of a real face. He remembered his own first efforts in drawing, and one day brought along a sketchbook he had kept as a boy and showed the children a delightful drawing of a grasshopper he had made at fourteen. Later, Hannah visited Blake's rooms in Fountain Court with her father. She always remembered the wonderful things she saw hanging on the walls there.

As dusk fell, Blake loved to stand at the door of the Linnells' cottage and gaze at the tranquil scene, or walk up and down in the garden, listening to the soft lowing of the cows from the neighboring farm. And when it was time to leave, if the night was cold, Mrs. Linnell would wrap him in an old shawl and send a servant with a lantern to light his and Palmer's way across the heath.

But there were times, and these now ominously frequent, when poor health prevented Blake from making the trip to Hampstead:

Dear Sir,

I have had another desperate Shivering Fit; it came on yesterday afternoon after as good a morning as I ever experienced. It began by a gnawing Pain in the Stomach, & soon spread a deathly feel over all the limbs, which brings on the shivering fit, when I am forced to go to bed, where I contrive to get into a little perspiration, which takes it quite away. It was night when it left me, so I did not get up, but just as I was going to rise this morning, the shivering fit attacked me again & the pain, with its accompanying deathly feel. I got again into a perspiration, & was well, but so much weaken'd that I am still in bed. This entirely prevents me from the pleasure of seeing you on Sunday at Hampstead, as I fear the attack again when I am away from home.

> I am, dear Sir,
> Yours sincerely,
> William Blake

Friday evening
May 19, 1826

Earlier that spring, the *Illustrations of the Book of Job* were completed and sent to the printer. A little over three hundred copies were printed. Though friends and dealers attempted to sell the book, the response was moderate at

The Whirlwind of Lovers, *c. 1824–27, the most highly finished of the seven large engravings to* Dante's Divine Comedy *begun by Blake during his final illness.*

best – barely more than thirty copies were sold during Blake's lifetime. Some buyers complained about the old-fashioned style of the engravings, "little calculated to take with admirers of modern engraving." Others complained about the binding, which was tight and pinched the paper. No profits were realized from the venture, and for years afterward, Linnell kept the unbound sheets in his workroom and had a book bound when an order came in.

When he was well enough, Blake worked on the illustrations to Dante's *Divine Comedy* in the large folio notebook Linnell had given him. He made 102 watercolor designs and several engravings, finishing them in varying degrees; but he failed to complete the massive project.

The "shivering fits" had grown progressively worse. He was visited by Doctor Thornton and took medicines, but nothing helped. By the end of 1826, Linnell had become so alarmed that he suggested to the Blakes that they move in rent-free to his house in Cirencester Place, where he could better see to their needs. However, by this time Blake was so frail that the mere thought of such a move put him in "a state of terrible fear."

Two of his dear friends had recently died – Fuseli in 1825, and John Flaxman in 1826. On being informed of Flaxman's death, he said simply, with a smile, "I thought I should have gone first." And then added, "I cannot think of Death as more than the going out of one room into another."

It is likely that Blake's final illness was inflammatory bowel disease, leading ultimately to liver failure. The disease may have been brought on by the long years of breathing in copper fumes as he worked on the etching of the copper plates for his engravings and Illuminated Books.

In April 1827, Blake wrote to his old friend George Cumberland, thanking him for his efforts to find orders for the Job illustrations, and promising to finish the engraving of the little visiting card Cumberland had commissioned from him. It was to be his last engraving.

Dear Cumberland,
I have been very near the Gates of Death & have returned very weak & an Old Man feeble & tottering, but not in Spirit & Life, not in the Real Man The Imagination which Liveth for Ever. In that I am stronger & stronger as this Foolish Body decays. I thank you for the Pains you have taken with Poor Job. . . .
   The Little Card I will do as soon as Possible but when you Consider that I have been reduced to a Skeleton from which I am slowly recovering you will I hope have Patience with me.
   Flaxman is gone & we must All soon follow, every one to his Own Eternal House, Leaving the Delusive Goddess Nature & her Laws to get into Freedom from all Law of the Members into the Mind, in which

Mr. Cumberland's Card, 1827.
Images of death and rebirth
inform the design.

every one is King & Priest in his own House. God send it so on Earth as
it is in Heaven.

I am, Dear Sir, Yours Affectionately,
William Blake

In that same month, William and Catherine, for the last time, took out the
copper plates for *Songs of Innocence and of Experience* and printed off a copy for
a friend, who had requested it. Nearly forty years had passed since they first
printed *Songs of Innocence*, back when they were both in the blush of youth.
And though William was now aged and ill, those copper plates gleamed still,
and the vision they contained remained unchanged.

William was well enough to visit the Linnell family one last time at the
beginning of July. The visit brought on a relapse, and the following week, in his
final letter to Linnell, he wrote, "I find I am not as well as I thought. I must not
go on in a youthful style."

Linnell looked in on William and Catherine frequently as the summer pro-
gressed and his friend's health declined. On August 10, he made a brief entry in
his journal: "To Mr. Blake. Not expected to live."

Bolstered up on pillows in his bed, Blake continued to work until the end.
Frederick Tatham, one of the young artists he had met through Linnell, and
later the author of one of the earliest biographies of Blake, had commissioned
a colored print of the design *The Ancient of Days*, which had first appeared as the
frontispiece to Blake's poem *Europe* in 1794. It had always been one of Blake's
favorite images, and during his final days he devoted himself to completing this

The Ancient of Days, *frontispiece to Blake's poem* Europe, 1794. *He colored this copy for Frederick Tatham during his last days.*

final copy. He would work on it awhile, then hold it at arm's length to study it.

"There," he said finally, casting it aside. "That will do. I cannot mend it."

Catherine sat by the bed, his faithful companion, his closest friend and confidant. It had been forty-five years ago, that very month, that they had been married.

"Stay, Kate," he said to her now. "Keep just as you are – I will draw your portrait – for you have ever been an angel to me." He told her that they could never be parted, that he would always be with her. Then he lay back on the bed. Soon, he began to sing songs of joy that seemed to flow spontaneously from his lips. "They are not mine, my beloved," he told her. "No – they are not mine."

At six o'clock that evening – August 12, 1827 – William Blake passed peacefully away. A neighbor, who had come to aid Catherine, was there at the end and said, "I have been at the death not of a man, but of a blessed angel."

Shortly after Blake's death, eighteen-year-old George Richmond, the youngest of the Ancients, happened to call. He kissed Blake as he lay in death upon the bed and closed his eyes "to keep the vision in."

Three days later, he wrote to Samuel Palmer:

My Dear Friend,

Lest you should not have heard of the Death of Mr. Blake I have written this to inform you – He died on Sunday Night at 6 O'clock in a most glorious manner. He said He was going to that Country he had all his Life wished to see & expressed Himself Happy hoping for Salvation through Jesus Christ – Just before he died his Countenance became fair – His eyes brighten'd and he burst out Singing of the things he saw in Heaven. In truth he Died like a Saint as a person who was standing by Him Observed. He is to be buried on Friday at 12 in the morning – Should you like to go to the Funeral – If you should there will be room in the Coach.

Yrs affectionately
G Richmond

CHAPTER SIXTEEN

CATHERINE: CONSULTING MR. BLAKE

I HAVE SAID TO THE WORM:
THOU ART MY MOTHER & MY SISTER

ILLIAM BLAKE WAS BURIED IN AN UNMARKED GRAVE IN Bunhill Fields. George Richmond, Edward Calvert, Frederick Tatham, his younger brother Arthur, and Catherine were present. Linnell, who did not approve of the Church of England service said at graveside, did not attend.

Still, he looked to the welfare of the grieving widow. He paid for the funeral, settled her accounts at Fountain Court, and invited her to live at his London studio. There, for a modest income, she served as housekeeper for a time. When the Linnell family moved to Porchester Terrace the following April, Catherine went to live with Frederick Tatham and his wife, "whose domestic arrangements

Catherine Blake, 1828, by George Richmond, from a drawing from the life by Frederick Tatham.

were entirely undertaken by her." Finally, in 1831, she moved into lodgings of her own at 17 Charlton Street.

Catherine was not alone, however. She said that William came to her for two or three hours every day. "He took his chair and talked to her, just as he would have done had he been alive." She had no inheritance beyond the wealth of William's Illuminated Books, copper plates, paintings, and manuscripts. She provided for herself by selling some of these to purchasers sent by Linnell, Richmond, and others concerned for her welfare. In addition, she printed new copies of several of William's books and hand-colored others. But she always refused to part with anything "until she had the opportunity of consulting Mr. Blake."

On October 18, 1831, Catherine Blake died. In her final hours, she was peaceful and calm, "repeating texts of scripture, and calling continually to her William, as if he were only in the next room, to say she was coming to him, and would not be long now."

On her death, all of Blake's prints, manuscripts, and copper plates fell into the hands of Frederick Tatham. This, despite the fact that Blake's sister, his sole surviving relative and the natural heir to his property, was living in a state of dire poverty. Relations between Linnell and Tatham deteriorated as Tatham attempted to secure possession of the Dante watercolors and engravings, which Linnell, in fact, had commissioned and paid for.

Over the next thirty years, Tatham turned a tidy profit selling off Blake's prints and drawings. He joined the Irvingites, a small fundamentalist sect, and, fired by religious zeal, destroyed an untold number of Blake's plates, drawings, and manuscripts.

We must be thankful for what remains, and grateful to those who preserved the memory of the man and his works through the decades of neglect that followed his death. Among those works – the paintings and engravings and Illuminated Books – was a little picture book of eighteen pages "For Children," printed by William and Catherine on their wooden press in Lambeth in 1793. It is a small uncolored book, spare of words, couched in mystery, yet within its narrow compass it contains the whole.

"What is Man?" it asks with its opening image, the vision of a cocoon as a swaddled child asleep on an oak leaf. Are we "worms of sixty winters," it seems to ask, or creatures called to transformation? Each small creative act we perform is a crack in the wall of the cocoon that encloses us, a faint tap against the inner side of the shell that surrounds us. To live creatively is to break the cocoon and loose the winged life within.

William Blake was one who struggled all his life against the constraints of the cocoon. The works he created were the wings on which he finally flew free. The example of his life and the vision of his work continue to inspire us to do the same.

SOURCE NOTES

All quotations from Blake's work are taken from *The Complete Writings of William Blake*, edited by Geoffrey Keynes.

All other quotations, except where noted, are from *Blake Records*, Second Edition, edited by G.E. Bentley, Jr., an invaluable chronological record of all contemporary documents relating to Blake's life, including the early biographical accounts by Benjamin Heath Malkin, Henry Crabb Robinson, John Thomas Smith, Alan Cunningham, and Frederick Tatham.

Books included in the bibliography are cited simply by author and title in the notes.

Chapter 1
The quote about the Blakes and the Fetter Lane Chapel is by William Muir (p. 10). It and the information on Catherine Blake's Moravian background are taken from the article "Recovering the Lost Moravian History of William Blake's family," by Ken Davies and Marsha Keith Schuchard in *Blake/An Illustrated Quarterly*, Summer 2004.

Chapter 2
The slogan "Famine decked in sackcloth" (p. 15) is cited in E.P. Thompson, *The Making of the English Working Class* (London: Victor Gollanz, 1963).

Chapter 3
Fuseli's interchange with his students (p. 32) is from Harold Bruce, *William Blake in This World* (New York: Harcourt, Brace and Company, 1925).

The quote "I never heard boys cry so" (p. 35) is cited in George Rudé, *Hanoverian London, 1714–1808*.

Chapter 5

The experiment with the workhouse children of St. James and its possible influence on Blake's work are detailed in Stanley Gardner, *The Tyger, the Lamb, and the Terrible Desart.*

The information on the details of Blake's techniques in Illuminated Printing is from Joseph Viscomi, *Blake and the Idea of the Book.*

The Jacob Boehme quote "Art has not written this, but all was ordered according to the direction of the Spirit . . ." (p. 59) is from *The Confessions of Jacob Boehme*, edited by W. Scott Palmer (New York: Harper & Brothers, 1954). The quotes "and not return to God . . ." and "Now I go to Paradise" are both cited in Rufus Jones, *Spiritual Reformers in the 16th and 17th Centuries.*

Chapter 6

The phrase "steam mill mad" (p. 65) is from Matthew Boulton as cited in Jacob Bronowski, *William Blake, 1757–1827: A Man Without a Mask.*

The quotes "While the engine works, the people must work . . ." (p. 66) and "If they will invent machines . . ." (p. 67) are cited in Kirkpatrick Sale, *Rebels Against the Future: The Luddites and Their War on the Industrial Revolution.*

The quote about "inferior children" (p. 71) is from Sarah Trimmer and is cited in Stanley Gardner, *Blake's Innocence and Experience Retraced* (New York: St. Martin's Press, 1986).

Chapter 7

Blake's response to the impact of the industrial revolution on art is discussed in Saree Makdisi's book, *William Blake and the Impossible History of the 1790s.*

The quote from Dr. Buchan on the swaddling of infants (p. 76) is cited in Stanley Gardner, *The Tyger, the Lamb, and the Terrible Desart.*

Chapter 8

The Robert Southey quote "Everything about that man is good . . ." (p. 86) is cited in Peter Ackroyd, *Blake.*

Chapter 9

Samuel's Palmer's remark on how Thomas Butts "stood between the greatest designer in England and the Workhouse" (p. 105) is from *The Letters of Samuel Palmer*, edited by Raymond Lister (Oxford: Clarendon Press, 1974).

Chapter 11

The discussion of the Luddite Rebellion is drawn largely from Kirkpatrick Sale, *Rebels Against the Future*.

Chapter 12

For more on Blake's response as an artist to the industrial revolution, see Morris Eaves, *The Counter-arts Conspiracy: Art and Industry in the age of Blake*.

Blake's quote "They pity me ..." (p. 139) is from Alexander Gilchrist, *Life of William Blake, "Pictor Ignotus."*

Chapter 13

The Varley quote "All these troubles . . ." (p. 148) is cited in Mona Wilson, *The Life of William Blake*.

The Varley quote "I am feeling all right . . ." is cited in Raymond Lister, *William Blake: An Introduction to the Man and His Work*.

Chapter 14

The quote from *The Pilgrim's Progress* by John Bunyan is from the Oxford World Classics edition, edited by W.R. Owens (Oxford: Oxford University Press, 1998).

The quote on Blake as one who "ennobled poverty . . ." (p. 165) is from Samuel Palmer. Both it and the quote "That is heaven" are from Alexander Gilchrist, *Life of William Blake, "Pictor Ignotus."*

Chapter 15

The Palmer quote "To walk with him in the country . . ." (p. 168) and the words of the neighbor on Blake's death (p. 175) are from Alexander Gilchrist, *Life of William Blake, "Pictor Ignotus."*

SELECTED BIBLIOGRAPHY

Blake's Works

The Complete Writings of William Blake, edited by Geoffrey Keynes. London: Oxford University Press, 1966. For many years, this was the standard edition of Blake's work. Keynes has attempted to regularize Blake's often erratic punctuation.

The Complete Poetry and Prose of William Blake, edited by David Erdman. Berkeley: University of California Press, 1982. This edition preserves Blake's original spelling and punctuation.

The Illuminated Books of William Blake, general editor David Bindman. Princeton: Princeton University Press, 1991–95. These six magnificent volumes, published by the Blake Trust, reproduce facsimiles of all Blake's Illuminated Books in their full-colored splendor.

Blake's Job: William Blake's Illustrations of the Book of Job, with an introduction and commentary by S. Foster Damon. New York: E.P. Dutton & Co., 1969.

Other Works

Ackroyd, Peter. *Blake*. London: Sinclair-Stevenson, 1995.

Bentley, G.E. Jr. *Blake Records*, Second Edition. London and New Haven: Yale University Press, 2004.

Bentley, G.E. Jr. *The Stranger from Paradise: A Biography of William Blake*. London and New Haven: Yale University Press, 2001.

Bindman, David. *William Blake: His Art and Times*. New Haven and Toronto: The Yale Center for British Art and the Art Gallery of Ontario, 1982.

Blackstone, Bernard. *English Blake*. Cambridge: Cambridge University Press, 1949.

Bronowski, Jacob. *William Blake, 1757–1827: A Man Without a Mask*. London: Penguin, 1944.

Damon, S. Foster. *A Blake Dictionary*. New York: Dutton, 1971.

Eaves, Morris. *The Counter-arts Conspiracy: Art and Industry in the Age of Blake*. Ithaca: Cornell University Press, 1992.

Erdman, David. *Blake: Prophet against Empire*. Princeton: Princeton University Press, 1954.

Essick, Robert. *William Blake, Printmaker*. Princeton: Princeton University Press, 1980.

Frye, Northrop. *Fearful Symmetry*. Princeton: Princeton University Press, 1947.

Gardner, Stanley. *The Tyger, the Lamb, and the Terrible Desart*. London: Cygnus Arts, 1998.

George, M. Dorothy. *London Life in the Eighteenth Century*. London: Kegan Paul, 1925.

Gilchrist, Alexander. *Life of William Blake, "Pictor Ignotus."* London: Macmillan, 1863. Reprint, ed. Ruthven Todd. London: Dent, 1945.

Jones, Rufus. *Spiritual Reformers in the 16th and 17th Centuries*. London: Macmillan, 1914. Reprint, Gloucester: Peter Smith, 1971.

King, James. *William Blake: His Life*. London: Weidenfeld and Nicolson, 1991.

Lister, Raymond. *William Blake: An Introduction to the Man and His Work*. London: G. Bell and Sons, 1968.

Makdisi, Saree. *William Blake and the Impossible History of the 1790s*. Chicago: University of Chicago Press, 2003.

Marshall, Dorothy. *English People in the Eighteenth Century*. London: Longmans, Green and Co., 1956.

Raine, Kathleen. *William Blake*. London: Thames and Hudson, 1970.

Rudé, George. *Hanoverian London, 1714–1808*. Berkeley: University of California Press, 1971.

Sale, Kirkpatrick. *Rebels Against the Future: The Luddites and Their War on the Industrial Revolution*. Cambridge: Perseus Publishing, 1995.

Schorer, Mark. *William Blake: The Politics of Vision*. New York: Vintage, 1959.

Thompson, E.P. *Witness Against the Beast*. New York: New Press, 1993.

Viscomi, Joseph. *Blake and the Idea of the Book*. Princeton: Princeton University Press, 1993.

Wilson, Mona. *The Life of William Blake*. London: Rupert Hart-Davis, 1948.

ILLUSTRATION CREDITS

Prologue and chapter heads. *For Children: The Gates of Paradise*, line engravings by William Blake. Copy D, 1793. The Rosenwald Collection, The Rare Book and Special Collections Division, The Library of Congress.

Page

5: *London at Night*, 1760, engraving by Slader after Fairholt, 1841. Robarts Library for the Humanities and Social Sciences, University of Toronto.

6: *In Bloomsbury Square*, 1787, engraving by R. Pollard and F. Jukes after E. Davis. Ibid.

7: *Golden Square*, from a print by Sutton Nicholls, 1754. Ibid.

9: 28 Broad Street, Golden Square. G.E. Bentley, Jr. Blake Collection, Victoria University Library (Toronto).

18: *Head of a Damned Soul*, engraving by William Blake after John Henry Fuseli, 1787–88. Copyright © The Trustees of the British Museum.

19: Holding and using the Graver, from Abraham Bosse, *De la Manière de Graver*, Paris, 1645. Thomas Fisher Rare Book Library, University of Toronto.

21: *Portrait of Henry III from his Monument*, line engraving by Blake. From Richard Gough, *Sepulchral Monuments of Great Britain*, 1786. Collection of Robert N. Essick. Copyright © 2006 the William Blake Archive. Used with permission.

23: *Body of Edward I in his coffin*, pen and sepia wash drawings by William Blake c. 1774. The Society of Antiquaries of London.

24: *Joseph of Arimathea Among the Rocks of Albion*, line engraving by Blake, 2nd state, 1773, c. 1810. Collection of Robert N. Essick. Copyright © 2006 the William Blake Archive. Used with permission.

27: *Drawing from Life at the Royal Academy* (Somerset House), by Thomas Rowlandson. Royal Academy of Arts, London.

30: *Glad Day*, line engraving by William Blake, c. 1803/1810. Rosenwald Collection Image © 2005 Board of Trustees National Gallery of Art, Washington.

35: *Attack on Newgate*, anon. engraving, c. 1780. Robarts Library for the Humanities and Social Sciences, University of Toronto.

38: Portrait of the young Blake, pencil drawing by Catherine Blake. Fitzwilliam Museum, Cambridge.

42: Wooden Rolling Press. Science Museum/Science & Society Picture Library.

44: *Study of a Youth*, by William Blake, possibly of Robert Blake, c. 1780. Black chalk. Copyright © The Trustees of the British Museum.

51: Fragment of canceled plate, *America: A Prophecy* (recto), 1793. Rosenwald Collection, Image © 2005 Board of Trustees, National Gallery of Art, Washington.

53: *Songs of Innocence*, colored relief etching by William Blake, title page, 1794. From *Songs of Innocence and of Experience*, Copy C. The Rosenwald Collection, The Rare Book and Special Collections Division, The Library of Congress.

55: "Nurse's Song." Colored relief etching by William Blake, 1794. From *Songs of Innocence and of Experience*. London, W. Blake, 1794. Copy Z. The Rosenwald Collection, The Rare Book and Special Collections Division, The Library of Congress.

57: *The Book of Thel*, colored relief etching by William Blake. Copy O. London, 1789. The Rosenwald Collection, The Rare Book and Special Collections Division, The Library of Congress.

62: "23 Hercules Rd.," pencil sketch by Frederick Adcock. Guildhall Library, Corporation of London.

65: *A Weaver's Workshop*, by J. Dircksz van Oudenrogge (1622–53). Rafael Valls Limited.

67: *Mule Spinning*, engraving by J.W. Lowry after T. Allom, 1835. Gerstein Science Information Centre Library, University of Toronto.

69: *Iron Works for Casting Cannon*, Severn Gorge, Coalbrookdale, 1788, engraving by Wilson Lowry after painting by George Robertson. Robarts Library for the Humanities and Social Sciences, University of Toronto.

70: *Joseph Johnson*, engraving by William Sharp after portrait by Moses Haughton, c. 1800. This item is reproduced by permission of *The Huntington Library, San Marino, California.*

76: *Songs of Experience*, colored relief etching by William Blake, title page, London, 1794. From *Songs of Innocence and of Experience*, Copy Z. The Rosenwald Collection, The Rare Book and Special Collections Division, The Library of Congress.

77: "The Chimney Sweeper," colored relief etching by William Blake, from *Songs of Experience*, Copy Z. The Rosenwald Collection, The Rare Book and Special Collections Division, The Library of Congress.

79: Inking, wiping, and printing engravings. From Abraham Bosse, *Traicté des manières de graveur en taille douce*. Paris, 1645. Thomas Fisher Rare Book Library, University of Toronto.

81: Edward Young, *Night Thoughts*, (p. 16), line engraving by Blake, 1797. G.E. Bentley, Jr. Blake Collection, Victoria University Library (Toronto).

84: *Malevolence*, watercolor with pen by William Blake, 1799. Philadelphia Museum of Art: Gift of Mrs. William Thomas Tonner, 1964.

87: *John Flaxman modelling his bust of William Hayley*, c. 1791–92, oil painting by George Romney. Yale Center for British Art, Paul Mellon Collection, USA/ Bridgeman Art Library.

89: Thomas Hayley medallion, engraving by Blake after Howard of the medallion by Flaxman, for Hayley's *Essay on Sculpture*, 1800. G.E. Bentley, Jr. Blake Collection, Victoria University Library (Toronto).

91: Blake's Cottage, Felpham. Kenneth Gravett, New Malden, Surrey.

92: *Geoffrey Chaucer*, tempera by Blake, c. 1800. Manchester City Art Gallery.

94: William Blake, self-portrait, c. 1803. Pencil and wash. Collection of Robert N. Essick. Copyright © 2006 the William Blake Archive. Used with permission.

96: *The Dog*, engraving by Blake for Hayley's *Ballads*, 1805. G.E. Bentley, Jr. Blake Collection, Victoria University Library (Toronto).

103: 17 South Molton St., Westminster. G.E. Bentley, Jr. Blake Collection, Victoria University Library (Toronto).

105: Portrait of Thomas Butts, on ivory by William Blake, 1801. Copyright © The Trustees of the British Museum.

107: *The Lord answering Job from the Whirlwind*, watercolor by Blake, c. 1803–05. The National Gallery of Scotland.

110: *Milton*, colored relief etching by W. Blake, Copy D. London, 1804. The Rosenwald Collection, The Rare Book and Special Collections Division, The Library of Congress.

115: *Death's Door*, white-line engraving by Blake, 1805. Collection of Robert N. Essick. Copyright © 2006 the William Blake Archive. Used with permission.

117: *Death's Door*, engraved by Schiavonetti after Blake's design for Blair's *Grave*, 1808. G.E. Bentley, Jr. Blake Collection, Victoria University Library (Toronto).

119: *Pilgrimage to Canterbury*, oil painting by Thomas Stothard, Jr. 1806–07. Tate Gallery, London/Art Resource, NY.

119: *Chaucer's Canterbury Pilgrims*, engraving by Blake, 5th state, 1810. Collection of Robert N. Essick. Copyright © 2006 the William Blake Archive. Used with permission.

120: *The Counsellor, King, Warrior, Mother and Child in the Tomb*, engraved by Schiavonetti after Blake's design for Blair's *Grave*, 1808. G.E. Bentley, Jr. Blake Collection, Victoria University Library (Toronto).

124: *The Penance of Jane Shore*, watercolor by William Blake, 1793. Tate Gallery, London/Art Resource, NY.

127: *Chaucer's Canterbury Pilgrims* (detail of image on p. 119).

130: Rawfold's Mill. Yorkshire. Robarts Library for the Humanities and Social Sciences, University of Toronto.

135: *Mrs. Blake*, portrait in pencil by William Blake. Tate Gallery, London/Art Resource, NY.

137: Wedgwood Ware, by William Blake, 1817. Plate 6. By courtesy of the Wedgwood Museum Trustees, Barlaston, Staffordshire (England).

139: *Lady Charlotte Susan Maria Bury* (née Campbell), engraving by K. Mackenzie after unknown artist, 1810. National Portrait Gallery, London.

141: *Jerusalem*, colored relief etching by William Blake, Copy E, frontispiece, 1804–20. © Yale Center for British Art, Paul Mellon Collection, USA.

143: *Jerusalem*, colored relief etching by William Blake, title page, Copy E, 1804–20. © Yale Center for British Art, Paul Mellon Collection, USA.

147: *Portrait of Blake*, by John Linnell, 1820. Pencil. Fitzwilliam Museum, Cambridge.

150: Visionary Heads of *William Wallace and Edward I*, by Blake, 1819. Pencil. Collection of Robert N. Essick. Copyright © 2006 the William Blake Archive. Used with permission.

151: *The Ghost of a Flea*, tempera on panel by William Blake, c. 1819–20. Tate Gallery, London/Art Resource, NY.

153: Four Woodcuts by Blake for Thornton's *Virgil*, 1821 (cuts 6–9). G.E. Bentley, Jr. Blake Collection, Victoria University Library (Toronto).

157: No. 3 Fountain Court. From *Art Journal*, IV (1858).

160: *Illustrations of the Book of Job*, engraving by Blake, pl. 1, *Thus did Job continually*, 1826. G.E. Bentley, Jr. Blake Collection, Victoria University Library (Toronto).

161: *Illustrations of the Book of Job*, engraving by Blake, pl. 21, *So the Lord blessed the latter end of Job more than the beginning*, 1826. (Ibid.)

163: Samuel Palmer, self-portrait in chalk, c. 1826. Ashmolean Museum, University of Oxford, UK / Bridgeman Art Library.

167: *William Blake at Hampstead, c. 1825*, pencil drawing by John Linnell. Fitzwilliam Museum, Cambridge.

168: *John Linnell*, pencil drawing by William Blake, 1825. Rosenwald Collection, Image © 2005 Board of Trustees, National Gallery of Art, Washington.

171: *The Whirlwind of Lovers*, engraving by Blake for Dante's *Divine Comedy* c. 1824–7. G.E. Bentley, Jr. Blake Collection, Victoria University Library (Toronto).

173: *George Cumberland's Card*, engraving by Blake, 1827. Collection of Robert N. Essick. Copyright © 2006 the William Blake Archive. Used with permission.

174: *The Ancient of Days*, colored relief etching by William Blake, 1827. The Whitworth Art Gallery, The University of Manchester.

177: *Portrait of Catherine Blake*, pencil sketch by George Richmond. © Yale Center for British Art, Paul Mellon Collection, USA.

Front endpapers: *Songs of Innocence*, title page, from *Songs of Innocence and of Experience*, Copy C. The Rosenwald Collection, The Rare Book and Special Collections Division, The Library of Congress.
"The Lamb," London, W. Blake, 1794. From *Songs of Innocence and of Experience*, Copy Z. Ibid.

Back endpapers: "The Tyger," London, W. Blake, 1794. From *Songs of Innocence and of Experience*, Copy Z. The Rosenwald Collection, The Rare Book and Special Collections Division, The Library of Congress.
Songs of Experience, title page, From *Songs of Innocence and of Experience*, Copy Z. Ibid.

INDEX

The Tyger

Tyger Tyger, burning bright,
In the forests of the night:
What immortal hand or eye,
Could frame thy fearful symmetry?

In what distant deeps or skies
Burnt the fire of thine eyes!
On what wings dare he aspire!
What the hand, dare seize the fire!

And what shoulder, & what art,
Could twist the sinews of thy heart?
And when thy heart began to beat,
What dread hand? & what dread feet?

What the hammer? what the chain,
In what furnace was thy brain?
What the anvil? what dread grasp,
Dare its deadly terrors clasp!

When the stars threw down their spears
And water'd heaven with their tears:
Did he smile his work to see?
Did he who made the Lamb make thee?

Tyger Tyger burning bright,
In the forests of the night:
What immortal hand or eye,
Dare frame thy fearful symmetry?